AFTER THE FALL

BY

DR. ALHASAN SISAWO CEESAY, MD

© 2014 by Dr. Alhasan Sisawo Ceesay, MD

All rights reserved. No part from this book may be reproduced in any form without written permission from the publisher, except by a reviewer who may quote passages in a review to be printed in a newspaper or magazine.

FIRST PRINTING

PUBLISH KUNSA.COM

INSCRIBED TO

My Parents, Wife and Children, Teachers, Friends, Colchester Friends of Manding Charitable Trust UK and Friends of Manding Alpena, Michigan, USA; and the downtrodden

African presidents should hold dear in mind that only good deed will soften and cushion their meteoric fall which almost always comes at unexpected time and tide.

Dr. Alhasan S. Ceesay, MD

## Preface and acknowledgments

William Shakespeare told us that, "He who is low need fear no fall." Rising from the fall is where people differ and what brings new life to all involved. Africa reels with an endless number of people all of who were victims of presidents they voted and brought to power.

Nothing progresses in Africa for lapse or lack of passionate nationalistic leaders. Instead the continent is loaded with presidents and Prime Misters who are threats to her development. These despots are deceptive, ruthless forces that leave toxic legacies. We do not need strong leaders but only strong institutions to maintain freedom and democracy.

These heartless and ungrateful greedy beasts turn their bile and vile nature to the peasants even if it will sink Africa in other to remain in power for life. No wonder they fall in disgrace leaving the continent in ruins and more backward than she was during the colonial era. These effigies of injustice turn more barbaric and inhumane than the wildest beast on earth.

The African lion has kinder heart than devils on two legs calling themselves presidents. They cause mayhem and bloodshed and so blood removes their footprints on earth, which should have been foot prints on the sand of time that a despondent seeing could take heart.

This work is about being a positive contributing member of society no matter where you may find yourself. It tries to shed reason why we need ignite the spirit and embers of giving not only to illuminate an others' life but to remove dark and despondent moments from those needy hearts.

In so doing we let hope and light triumph over darkness and hence allow peace to transcend earth. Very inspirational characters are presented in hope of motivating you to do good causes waiting for your mark. In the mean time allow me express profound gratitude to my wife and children for bearing and persevering patiently through with me in thick and thin during my drive to bring medical aid and service to villagers.

Also I am immensely thankful to illustrious lawyer Ousainu Darboe, Alhaj Kebba Saneh, Lorna Robinson, Eliza Jones, Dr. Laurel Spooner, Dr. Barbra Murray, Dr. Phil Spooner, Dr. Richard Murray, Dr. Malkaight Singh, Cloyd Ramsey, Howard Riggs, Rita Riggs, Dr. Charles Egli, Dr. Cooper Milner, Dr. Nelson Herron, Deidre O'Leary, Margaret Cruise, Bill Cruise, Alison Cruise, Dr. Eunice Kahan, Dr. Betzabi Alison-Prager, Henry Valli, Fr. John Milner, Homer Shepard, Geraldine Shepard, Dr. Lamin J. Sisay, Dr. Sulayman S. Nyang, Bishops Masson & Coleman McGhee of the Episcopal Diocese of Michigan, Detroit, the Ceesay Committee Diocese of Michigan, Lois R.

Leonard, Rev. Walter White, Rev Huge White, Patricia Koblynski, Ishfaue Ahmed, Imran Khurum Ahmed, Mohamed Nasir, Ahmed Nizami, Abdinnisir Hassan, Faisal Alim, Abdal Rhaseed Suguelle, Noora Sugulle, Mahmud Adam, Ganem Al Hadied, Abdullah Shahim, Asiya Qadri, Yusuf Ali, and numerous others whose names are not mention but not forgotten.

I write to raise money for the building of a village hospital at Njawara, the Gambia. It is my hope that you would be inspired to join our dream of providing medical aid and service to Gambian villagers and children in the North Bank region.

Purchasing this book or donating in cash or kind would help bring our dream to fruition of Manding Medical Centre for a much needed healthcare delivery and hope to villagers, especially children who frequently die prematurely from childhood diseases because of lack of medical service.

Together we can catch a dream for the villager and children. Log onto: www. Friends of Manding gambimed, to learn more about our self-help village health project Manding Medical Centre at Njawara. Portions of proceed from sale of this work go to support goals of Manding Medical Centre.

In addition it will in due course offer scholarships to rural candidates wishing to read for a medical or an agricultural degree and return to serve in rural Gambia.

Dr. Alhasan S. Ceesay, MD

# Chapter 1
## Enemies of Peace, Truth and Law

From day that political parties where allowed to encroach into the minds of the people a very divisive element was irreversibly injected into life of the peasantry. Politicians like their colonial mentors capitalised upon the most indecent operative of divide and rule.

With this heinous tool African politicians used it effectively to the point of dragging tribal allegiance above nationhood and making party being sure way to job opportunity. This unravelled the tiniest amount of tranquillity that existed between the tribes who up to independence had old scores to settle.

Party ramblings and tribal affiliation were death knell to good governance in the continent. Most politicians mastered the art of double talking with two forked tongue. They promise heaven on earth during political rallies but in reality were laying traps and way they and theirs would make good living from blood of the peasantry.

Telling the truth, such as letting voters know that it would take decades of good governance, hard work, and true democratic system before Africa reaches a third of developmental state of the superpowers. There in fact no transparency, accountability and probity in Gambia.

## Dr. Alhasan Sisawo Ceesay, MD

The politicians rather promise to turn the country or place into the likes of Singapore or an eventual home of milk and honey for all who duel in it. They do not contribute to development of their people nor are they amenable to telling the truth.

Truth is the pillar of trust and development which was very lacking in the way politicians plan, and evaluate party achievements in nation building. They tell of highly exaggerated outcomes of their development plans and fill the place with prestigious homes and villas belonging to them and their chain of easy women.

The country's constitution is either over amended to suit their whims or completely abrogated to avoid penalties and rules therein. Eventually neither the president and his party, nor his tribe's men respect the rule of law. They and their relatives, friends and corrupt business men and operatives see themselves above the law of the state.

They assume being the state, it coffers belonging to them and the judiciary under their control. They empower themselves and a select arm of securities to carry out their dirty deeds of kidnappings, tortures, disappearances and even outright murder of any that opposes them or is perceived to differ from them and their thievery. Woe be tired you if you are an academic, who the president fears to be his likely replacement.

## After The fall

One President pride himself by threatening to send any who does not like him or way he runs the country to his five star hotel, which is his nasty acronym joke for high detention prison. Hence fear, terror and intimidation causes meekness and extreme obedience to the higher ups. With the masses weakened the rule of law is thrown out by the window and never to be mentioned for life of the junta in power.

The President fills most of the posts in the Army, Police, Immigration and Customs from members of his tribe. And to add fuel to a raging inferno the presidents gives these forces sweeping power over the citizenry. Brutality unleased by these presidential security is unmatched by any in human history.

Homes are looted, pilfered and occupants kidnapped, tortured to confess to crimes they never dreamt or committed before being killed or paraded before the public on their way to a heartless kangaroo court the next day. These bullies are then rewarded with promotions buttered by presence of cars and villas to repose with family. Soon these dawn bellies bigger than a tambour and as power corrupt they too soon set eye onto the presidency and organize a coup d'état to be the nation's God and to get the bigger share of national cake.

Dr. Alhasan Sisawo Ceesay, MD

Blood built that which brought them to power and blood brings it down. This vicious circle goes on almost endless because political life was being based upon falsehood instead of truth, justice, good governance and true democracy.

Some countries had as high as nineteen coups happening through a span of twenty years before finally accepting the need for a two term length of rule for any party rather than lifelong AK47 monarchs that indiscriminately kill its citizens.

Africa is said to have more of pseudo-politicians and that the continent reels from severe lack of statesmen. Africa has for the past seventy years exchanged one master for another with the outsider remaining in the shadows as they pull strings of installed puppets who now serve as masters over lives of the indigent.

These new puppets are adept in the art of inflating promises and raising false hopes in other to be selected again and again by yearning societies wishing to get out of poverty to improve life. These politicians lie with consummate ease before the electorate who childishly believe in their empty oratory. The oratory made ordinary citizens believe in the promise of turning country into Singapore, silicon vale, own factories and businesses that rake money to them.

## After The Fall

History teaches that rarely do politician following their passion to govern and do so purely for altruistic or idealistic reasons. The nature of the beast was to hide behind lofty ideals like democracy that represent interest of the people, but in essence the goal is to remain a wolf in sheep's clothing while garnering power and wealth from the flock they feed upon.

The election trail is strewed with cohesion and bribery to opponents. Gone are the days of statesmanship, honesty and passion to help relief their citizenry from misery. Politicians while on campaign trails talk about transparency, improving of social services, education, health, women empowerment and other false promises just to gain votes.

The ordinary man and woman in the street only want some relief and would work to improve their lives but the merciless empty-headed, corrupt politician's only cause is to blindfold the herd from reality while raking money from them even if that meant taking the last drop of blood from these innocent yearning to free themselves from painful lows wilting their lives.

Former south African President, Nelson Mandela reminds us thus, "In this new century, millions of people in the world's poorest countries remain imprisoned, enslaved and in chains.

They are trapped in the prison of poverty.

It is time to set them free." The discourse between the governing and opposition becomes academic pedantry. Manifestos yell, "A vote for us is a vote for you!"

## Dr. Alhasan Sisawo Ceesay, MD

The truth is history since independence shows that both are the same wolf in sheep clothing thinking they are cleverer than the rest whose support they need to ascend to the throne. The winner takes all. Opposition parties must heed Gandhi's counsel, "Be the change you want others to be."

The opponent tells its listeners that it believes in democracy and freedom and would be everyone's president because all belong to the same country. This dear reader is rubbish rhetoric's without passion or any statesmanship in its approach as the hidden agenda is to try and get the nation's bootie.

Meanwhile the government reverts to spying on the timorous flock to keep them not only in line but also under the ever-peering eyes of state in the name of national security. Telephones of opponents are tapped while CCTV cameras are installed in such areas to detect the slightest signs of discontent shown by those adverse to the ruling party.

Hence technology is wrongly used to stifle freedom of speech and movement without fear of arrest. CCTV cameras, pervasive bugging scrutinizes and records everything that happens in the domestic life of every opponent for daring to oppose or question the art of the president or boss.

Threats to prosecute exile citizens in the Diasporas critical of failing human rights among other shortcomings of the ruling government are to be arrested for painting ugly and unsavoury pictures of their countries. They deemed these exiles as evil members of society taking refuge abroad tarnishing the good work of national governments.

## After The Fall

Proponents of such draconian acts fail to accept that stifles freedom of speech lays dark dictatorial egg that hatches mayhem to hunt them. What goes round comes back to get us at our most vulnerable time. This is clearly manifested in the way most African dictators meet their ends. A government should be that of the people by the people and for the people.

No nation should be property of the president, his party or any tribe including his own tribe. In Africa, the president, army, his party and tribe rules at will till death meets them but never to be replaced through democratic means. These dictatorial presidents become Africa's' hidden monarchies giving lip service to civilized democratic ideals and governance.

A few tried their hands in unveiling their monarchical faces by becoming Emperors or even kings. These vermin's daily violate the human rights of opponents. When will African leaders put their greed and differences and unite for the common good of Africa?

Iron fisted authoritarian rulers and so called geo-politic strong men almost always end up being driven from power by soaring protest by their fed up populist who no longer accept corruption, lairs, deception, nepotism, and unemployment.

The leaders must see themselves as flag bearers of Africans and not become wolves in sheep clothing to their citizenry. They must not only uphold patriotism, respect the people but also must be willing to protect the lives and properties of Africa.

## Dr. Alhasan Sisawo Ceesay, MD

Africa lived under the yoke and den of colonials for over four hundred years and now its citizens suffer daily psychological and physical mutilation for purely being members of a tribe or opposing parties. First and foremost, there has to be a stop to such brutalities and a common sincere effort applied to correct injustice while practicing acceptable good governance.
I besiege my continent to seek to bring true democracy to the people instead of propagating ferment and tribal rule. It is making the youth frustrated and hopeless pushing them to risk their lives across the Mediterranean to seek greener pastures from hostile lands.
Africa must stop walking east while actually wrongly going west. In short no African nation belongs to any particular president, party or tribe. These ugly orgies of political irresponsibility end up irrationally decimating thousands and destroying the lives and property of millions. Independence now conjures up penal colonies of some dark ages ago.
Currently, Africans are not at ease with way they are governed. We ask why politician would blast our ears with dreams of turning the continent into the likes of Singapore or Silicon Valley while at the same time stifle freedom and development.
African politicians must break away from their current Subterfuge cocoon of selfishness and strive to be the state men everyone hoped. People need to safe, productive countries and live under dictatorships or besieged by the merciless rule of king AK47. Helping and not massacring people is buzzing phenomenon that promotes development of a region.

## After The Fall

In addition they must revert to being harbingers of development and progress expected of them. Africa must Innovate its people and stop staring at the abyss that buries her people in despair. It is said that the evil men do lives after them and the good is often interred with their bones. Plato reminds us that the following qualities are inherent requirement for a good state man. Such persons he said should have a good memory, quickness at learning, broadness of vision, elegance, and love of and affiliation to truth, morality, courage, and self-discipline. In the immediacy of common need of statesmanship and good governance I dream and cling to hope that African leaders would respect human rights and freedom of the people and also aspire to leave inspirational noble footprints for other generations to take heart and follow their revered examples.

Dr. Ceesay & Mr. Sisawo Ceesay
Father, December 1960

Dr. Alhasan Sisawo Ceesay, MD

## Chapter 2

## Starvation and Economic slavery

There is no doubt that economic slavery leads to starvation. In a continent starving from chronic need of good governance the people are bound to starve for lack of equipment to plough the land and good roads to transport their product to the market.

There is no competitive business in Africa as the President or his crony's monopolies all aspects of commerce where only bribery gets one to order or even purchase goods. No one competes with coffers of state which the president doles into his companies. Even ladies are complaining of the high cost from taxation levied upon them as vendors and petty traders. The only fairly usable roads are those frequented by the president and the rest are left unrepaired and worthless death traps for trucks plying to and from villages.

To add pepper to injury all able bodied men and women are obliged to offer free of charge at least two days work at the president's farms every week of the rainy season. Failing to work at the Oga's farm causes painful repercussions for the family head and his relatives. His annual taxation is increased and heartless revenue collectors seize his property to make of the difference.

## After The Fall

With a populace denied economic means slavery ensues. The rich become tsars over the peasantry and mouth pieces of the president. They offer wages that could not even feed a canary more over a normal African family of fifteen to twenty at minimal.

On top of which the desertification has rendered most arable farming land useless due erratic rain fall or no rain at all in some seasons. It does at times look like both nature and politician seem to concertedly conspire against hard working African farmers. Ninety nine percent of all climate changes and desertification are both man made hazards.

For lack of usable energy source villagers turn to cutting down trees for charcoal to cook and also sell or buy food and pay taxis. The high rate of decimations of forest wood for cooking and making furniture rendered the already tethering African forest extinct.

The industrial powers want cheap Africa wood to make furniture from but cared the least about their greedy use of this raw Africa natural gift they believed in-exhaustible. With the forest gone villagers now end up buying imported gas for cooking and very costly furniture from overseas. It is disheartening to see open spaces between villages that had thick forests days gone by.

Dr. Alhasan Sisawo Ceesay, MD

The total effect of being forced or needing to work at the president's farm without pay and the unavailability of alternative cash crops hardy enough to withstand desertification made life miserable for villagers.

The high unemployment rate added to gimmickry of business and the rich added and economic insult to injury for farmers.

Front: Fatou Dibba and Isatou Dibba

Back: Dr. Ceesay, Mrs. Fanatandin Tarawale,

(mother) holding Penda Fibba, and Babucarr Dibba

After The Fall

Chapter 3

The Solution and Way forward

To every problem there is a realistic solution. The way out of Africa's nightmare that affects the Gambia and her sister states lies squarely on freedom, education, hard work, agriculture, exploration and innovations. There is no beating about the bush when it comes to benefits of freedom and its ability to stimulate hidden talents.

A free society is a progressive one and if that freedom is allowed to gain deeper taproots backed by respect for the rule of law within a democratically ratified constitution nothing but advancement emanates. Either a pseudo or full blown slavery exists in the absence of freedom and democracy.

The two are inseparable inter linked for without the other either mayhem or slavery eats the soul of community of nations. Raw ignorance cannot persist as it is hindrance to development. The masses must be schooled through the provision of good schools and by encouraging people willing to be teachers to be trained and running the class rooms and not politicians or pseudo-educationists. Education is the earthly soul of a people.

## Dr. Alhasan Sisawo Ceesay, MD

Education must take into account the future of the next generation and offer them good start for them to have chance for a good start in life. Most African governments speak of improving education only to be found lacking inspirational and political will to do it but create party oriented curriculums where children and students have to literally sing praises to the ruler and his ministers to get head way in life.

To get to higher learning most have to bribe because children of the rich and politicians get first available spaces before the poor peasant's children do, no matter how brilliant and motivated those children turn out. Good governance ushers good programs and schools as it leaves no citizen aside.

Another solution to Africa's problem is none affordability of safe drinking and cooking water, good shelter or housing system, and electricity, backed by a proper modern healthcare delivery. Most of our rivers are amenable hydroelectricity production but the politicians rather eat the money than invest in such worthy and much needed facilities for the citizenry.

Rather they would buy well-polished, fifth hand me down dead generators, breakdown every quarter requiring engineers from abroad to come and do the repairs for lack of trained personnel in suitor.

## After The Fall

Instead of using money they stole to teach technicians and dam engineers the politician buys villas in Spain, Francis and now America. What is sadder about this is fact that the very shameless politician would turn around and ask these countries for monetary support in other to rung government of their states.

The average villager or citizen is hard working and the stolen monies could have been invested in facilitation of good liveable housing for the people. Well staffed hospital and health Centre should be adjunct to these villages connected with durable feeder roads not the footpaths that are not only unsafe but full of trenches that would not allow easy plying through of ambulances. Salaries must be worth the service rendered applied equally to all employees.

It is said that a hungry nation is a sick nation and that an empty bag cannot stand by itself. Agriculture is the bread basket of any human community and government should always give it high priority and openly meet farmers to learn from them and to know their need in other to be more productive. Africa has huge arable land waiting to be farmed but for lack of irrigation, good roads and bridges the villager still uses little plots passed onto them by their ancestors.

Dr. Alhasan Sisawo Ceesay, MD

In my village the simple hoe and cutlass still remain tools at hand. No tractors or combine harvesters hum their way to the fields in most of Africa. Mechanized farming is rare and very new in Africa in few places it exists.

Farmers should be provided with disease hardy commercial crops as alternative or in addition to ones they currently use for them to be able support family, pay school fees for their children and to have some semblance of a good life before dying. It is a shame note starvation still existing in a continent that could easily be the world's bread basket.

Government should train agriculturists and drainage technician to help the farmers make better use of the arable farms lying fallow because of lack of know how. Another element Africa is endowed is her mineral resources. There is so much off-shore as well as inland oil deposits in Africa that no citizen deserves to live life they are currently enduring. In addition Africa has abundant deposits of gold, diamond, iron ore, and a whole host minerals needed by industry that are still lying undisturbed deep in the ground.

Heads of states only allow foreign buccaneers to explore these and in return not only bribe their way in do so but re-siphoned the finish products to Africa at unaffordable cost to average citizens.

## After The Fall

Lastly but not the least what keeps a country interconnected are good infrastructure which allows free and easy movement of goods and people both for trading and even tourism. Roads most be made safe and durable for them to be cost worthy.

In Africa the backdoor contract makes meal of honesty and yields nothing poor workmanship that no one dare point out for fear of hurting the feelings of the big man at the helm. Hence new roads become full of potholes that even the best vehicle breaks in attempting to pass through.

Time is of asset but not in Africa for what need to take only one day trip would last five days during the rains and three in the dry season. The roads are just not worth the name given them. As mentioned above Africa would develop exponentially had there been correct electricity supply to the people.

Our black smiths, formers, carpenters, engineers and house whole used would bring development and provide source of living for the people. Rivers could be tapped for hydroelectricity production and irrigation to provide water to fields. This bird's eye view of solving Africa's current woes is just a start and it ushers in better future and more innovative community.

Dr. Alhasan Sisawo Ceesay, MD

## Chapter 4
### THE POLITICS OF THE TRIBE

There is nothing wrong with the tribe and its birth right of those who belong to one. What is sacrilegious about the tribe, especially in Africa, is it alignment with nepotism and political aggrandizing use of members of the tribe. Plato lecturing about innate human behaviour said, "If one is offered to choose out of all the customs in the world such as seemed to them the best, they would examine the whole number, and end by preferring their own; so convinced are they that their own usages far surpass those of all of them...such is men's wont herein; and Pindar was right when he said, "Law is the king over all."
Once a president is elected his tribe start to show obvious pomposity out right and desire to fl aunt laws with knowledge that little if any would be done to bring them to account for their unholy deeds.
Firstly, Africa must stop tribalism and corruption that accompany it. Secondly, where racism is sin, tribalism is Africa's cardinalsin. A despicable spiteful illness dwells in weak minds. The overt affiliation to tribe is the main source of corruption that buffers and buttresses nepotism in governments and the civil services in Africa.
In Africa and in most cases, as soon as a president forms Government the ball game rolling the vicious dice of tribalism shows its ugly head. His tribesmen start juggling and competing for recognition for cabinet positions or some high post in the Army and civil service.

## After The Fall

In the hope of guaranteeing his security, the president makes the common mistake of appointing a member of his tribe as Chief of Army Staff above many who might have better qualifications. Failing to go this chicken route, he may hire a foreign mercenary and appoint that as army head.

By the time the day is over all sectors and government departments ends up infected by cronies and cancerous tribal link or tentacles of African's socio-political virus. Henceforth, other tribes can only get their needs met through bribery and deception. These underlings have to pay their way for anything they want from simple permits to landing lucrative contracts.

Their talents and skills become irrelevant and only the "Whom you know qualification" can land them a job or get scholarship for their progeny. Government being the highest employer makes the people vulnerable to such heinous experiences in other to get on in life.

Tribalism has also been the source of many a conflict in Africa especially when the larger tribes refuse to share the meagre bread of state with the rest. Tribalism makes African presidents push for lifelong stay in power and in doing so personalises government.

It is my understanding that government is of the people, for the people and by the people. In Africa, it is the government of the president's tribesmen and all other citizens are subject to the caprices and whims of such nonentities. The country and resources belongs to the president who does with it whatever pleases him, his henchmen and tribe.

Dr. Alhasan Sisawo Ceesay, MD

Tribalism is the vanguard and root cause of a majority of the instabilities in the African continent. This was mirrored, as recently as, in the case of the Kenyan 2008 slaughter after the farce election results and likewise in the not long ago conflicts between the African Nation Congress and Zulu InKata during the anti apartheid days of the 1960s.

This cancer and that of lifelong presidencies have to be stamp out of our government before genuine democracy and progress is achieved for the good of our people. Through this Africa will be able to curb the external tinkering in our political affairs and economies.

To those who say asking for the above transformations tantamount to seeking incarnation of African minds and responsibilities.

I say that it is possible but one would in doing just that has to have plans with which to wake the African out of his slumber. Let me rebuff such arguments by categorically stating that there is nothing more disastrous for Africa than tribal intrusion into governance of any ruling party. It is criminal to condone such dark interferences to proper democratic practice.

Even Rip van Wrinkle woke up after twenty years somnolence. Let us say loudly, "No tribalism or rule by inept lifelong presidents for Africa," We must do away with these devils. We must work for Africa and humanity instead of paying allegiants to tribalism and dictatorial regimes that insult our integrity. Our governments must seek to make life better and as tolerable as possible for those who elected them to power.

After The Fall
Chapter 5
GOVERNMENT BY CONSENT

Government by the people and for the people should be rule of thumb for African governance. The clean majority will of the electorate must be the route to power and ruling of our nations. The people must be allowed to question their rulers, utilization of the nation's coffers, above all have a say in needed priority projects to ward off bias towards prestige oriented projects which eventually becomes nests for sources of corruption.
As it stands today, in most countries the incumbent always wins election by unheard of majority votes, which in the end stifles participation and leads to cycles of violence and mayhem.
Money wrongly dragged or siphoned from the meagre national till to buy weapons to maintain oneself in power in the name of national security could be properly used if elections are run fairly and open to all parties.
The reality on the ground is that the citizens with opposite views are either crushed through coercion, or bribery and outright refusal of proper registration documents.
Corrupt ruling parties undeniably breed corruption and retrogression to national development and causes great suffering in remaining in power.
These hidden modern slave masters do so by being vanguards or puppets of vying superpowers whose only interest is to rake away our mineral and natural resources for their people. These leaves us crumbs while taking the best out of our region at almost no price for the indigenous African.

## Dr. Alhasan Sisawo Ceesay, MD

Africa must embrace both economic and self-sufficiency in feeding, educating, sheltering itself through good governance and freedom of the people they rule. This can only be achieved if the governing allows the wish of the people to be sovereign and modem operandi.
Free society backed by freedom of choice over comes obstacles and bring development at faster rate than when under the yoke of slavery. Dark hearted politicians never deem this to be the case as progress sends them tumbling in an endless abyss.
Hence, the reason while they thread upon any who professes to lift the masses from oblivion.
The cornerstone of progress is that ability to explore freely the fullest extent of one's talents or skills without fear or interference of government. Africa is losing her intelligentsias to Europe and America because of constant intimidation by ruling regimes.
A country without good think tanks or sources of guiding academicians to tap from is mare hollow shells drifting with winds of geopolitics. Governing through the consent of the majority would, as it currently stands, call for reorientation of present African political minds from darkness to happy daylight to ascent to reality for the people of the continent.
This impels politicians to think passionately of the good of the people rather than power and wealth the seat anoints for consent intertwined with freedom of the people is indeed cornerstone of good governance and democracy. Is there any good in the current welter of ugly political nightmare?

## After The Fall

Unless there is true political power emanating from the consent of the majority of the populace there can be no end to political troubles, mischief, instability and the current mayhem Africa bitterly endures.
There is nothing more disastrous for the community than tribal intrusion into the running of a government. It is to my view criminal and such tribal interferences should not be condoned in proper democratic practice.
The world cannot wait for Africa to get her act together to be competitive and contributing positively to the good of her people and mankind. China and India, countries whose development sixty years ago where in similar state as Africa, are now fast ahead in development that brings basic relief to their citizens.
Why do our politicians continue to play greedy games with the farmers or voters that sent them to parliament? We do not need bloodshed to bring change but we do need statesmanship and aggressive common sense to retrieve our continent from the brink of disaster it currently faces. It is high time African leaders accept that the will of the people is sovereign and sacrosanct.
The African continent cannot continue on snail pace while the rest of mankind moves with leaps and bounce rocketing sky wise. To gain support of the masses African leaders must identify areas of need and feasible projects that would bring progress and self-reliance.
The people do not like puppet nor do they like being swung between geopolitical powers who's only interest lies in mineral and natural resources of the continent.

Dr. Alhasan Sisawo Ceesay, MD

The bottom line for governing any nation lies on gaining full consent of the people as will and politics of the masses encourages stability and pulsating development in any forward looking country. Refusing to heed the voices of the masses kills incentives and innovation and nerve tract of a country' development.

Mrs. Fatou Koma-Ceesay: UK 2015

Dr. Alhasan Sisawo Ceesay, MD

Chapter 6

BEYOND TRIBAL PITFALLS

Where racism is sin, tribalism is Africa's cardinal sin. A despicable spiteful illness dwells in weak minds. The overt affiliation to tribe is the main source of corruption that buffers and buttresses nepotism in governments and the civil services in Africa.

In Africa and in most cases, as soon as a president forms government the ball game rolling the vicious dice of tribalism shows its ugly head. His tribesmen start juggling and competing for recognition for cabinet positions or some high post in the Army and civil service.

In the hope of guaranteeing his security, the president makes the common mistake of appointing a member of his tribe as Chief of Army Staff above many who might have better qualifications.

Failing to go this chicken route, he may hire a foreign mercenary and appoint that as army head. By the time the day is over all sectors and government departments ends up infected by cronies and this cancerous African socio-political virus.

This is the abyss of African democracy or governance. Henceforth, other tribes can only get their needs met through bribery and deception. These underlings have to pay their way for anything they want from simple permits to landing lucrative contracts.

Their talents and skills become irrelevant and only the "Whom you know qualification" can land them a job or get scholarship for their progeny.

## After The Fall

Government being the highest employer makes the people vulnerable to such heinous experiences to get on in life. Tribalism has also been the source of many a conflict in Africa, especially where the larger tribes refuses to share the meager bread of state with the rest.

Tribalism makes African presidents push for lifelong stay in power and in doing so personalizes government. It is my understanding that government is of the people, for the people and by the people.

In Africa, it is the government of the president's tribesmen and all other citizens are subject to the caprices and whims of such nonentities. The country and resources belongs to the president who does with it whatever pleases him, his henchmen and tribe.

Tribalism is the vanguard and root cause of a majority of the instabilities in the African continent. This was mirrored, as recently as, in the case of the Kenyan 2008 slaughter after the farce election results and likewise in the not long ago conflicts between the African Nation Congress and Zulu Inkata during the anti apartheid days of the 1960s.

This cancer and that of lifelong presidencies have to be stamp out of our government before genuine democracy and progress is achieved for the good of our people. Through this Africa will be able to curb the external tinkering in our political affairs and economies. Some say asking for the above transformations tantamount to seeking incarnation of the African and responsibilities.

## Dr. Alhasan Sisawo Ceesay, MD

I say that it is possible but one would have to have plans with which to wake the African out of his slumber. Even Rip van Wrinkle woke up after twenty years somnolence. Let us say loudly, "No tribalism or rule by inept lifelong presidents for Africa".
We must do away with these devils. We must work for Africa and humanity instead of paying allegiants to tribalism and dictatorial regimes that insult our integrity. Our governments must seek to make life better and as tolerable as possible for those who elected them to power.

Dr. Ceesay displays his first book, 2002

# After The Fall

## Chapter 7
### A SUCCESSFUL MAN LEARNS FROM HIS MISTAKES

All humans make mistakes or are capable of making one. The difference in outcome of our errors is being able to accept that we erred and to learn from it to make better judgments next time. Some say my mistake was refusing to stay in the village mould and that I was too ambitious if not a grandiose psychopath pursuing Western ideals.

So far, I have been able to assail through most criticisms and completed university education despite it all. Some say I should not have left America to study medicine at A. M. Dogliotti, school of medicine in Monrovia, Liberia, West Africa or even attend the American university of the Caribbean at Montserrat in the West Indies.

Friends have on many occasions asked why I did not seek the Green card while a student in America or apply for the United Kingdom citizenship during my clinical clerkship rotation at Colchester, Essex.

My response then and even today is that I refrained from such a course because I love Africa and there is no place I rather be other than the Gambia. More over our people need our services more than any other place.

## Dr. Alhasan Sisawo Ceesay, MD

I love helping villagers and would do just that with my life in the time that God gave me on planet earth. In addition I am certain to fulfil my goal, with help of Manding Medical Centre, of providing medical aid to the villager. The end result of, dear reader, that error, if it be one, was it turned me into the doctor I am today for the villagers and the needy.

The road to that lofty end was long and difficult at times too slippery and steep to walk on. It was strewed with stagnation, starvation, and destitutions life. Hope you will agree that the end result was worth the means for family and country. It is no fanfare or path for the weak and none persistent person.

I suffered tremendously since my arrival in the UK, the so-called land of honey and milk of Europe. I faced series of evictions from flats, had been threatened with CCJ actions and a host of collection agents vying to lay hands on anything belonging to me to recoup money owed to either the RBS or BT. Life in this state was nerving, shameful and painful.

The mistake, which lead to this disheartening state, was that I came to the UK on a visitor's visa. The Home Office's refusal to reclassify my visa to a student visa landed me into hell on earth.

## After The Fall

Some asked if the struggle was worth the pain and dehumanization state I found myself at. My response had always been a resounding yes with a challenge for doubters to meet me in the Gambia upon my completing certification with the GMC three years hence. On my way home, I had two fellows discussing about me.

The other said that I was wrong in not listening as well as obeying my father's wish that I become a farmer instead of being immersed in some foreign ideology and system. The sensible one retorted by asking why they were the in UK and not farming in the Gambia.

He told his companion that Dr. Ceesay was spending himself for the future good of all Gambians for if his medical centre catches on it would be added valuable medical service to the Gambia and the Badibous in particular.

I met some Gambian at the Alexandra Park and they too suggested that think of returning since life had been nothing but a downward spiral for me since my coming to the UK.

I reminded them that if mountain climbers were scared of the height they wish conquered or mistakes others made in their attempts to climb those mountains, we would never assailed Mount Everest.

## Dr. Alhasan Sisawo Ceesay, MD

A mistake is a necessary lesson to learn from and to humble ourselves from the belief of being infallible. Our mistakes are eye openers to bigger gains. They may at first be bitter to swallow but if we learn from them we gain a lot of insight in future plans.

If the Manding Medical Centre and all it now provide the Gambia was a mistake then I pray to make a billion more similar sincere mistakes for mankind. It is said to err is human and to forgive divine. I hope those could not see beyond the tip of their noses could forgive me for refusing to stay in the village mould and pursue to the hilt what I believe to be worthy end for the Gambia, villagers and the downtrodden.

I am no angel and like you I am full of human imperfections. The difference between my critics and I is that I am a dreamer who never gives up dreaming and I am always ready to see the dreams come true to a positive beneficial reality for all of us. This is my way of leaving footprints on the sand of time so that beleaguered Gambians can muster courage and work for the development of the region.

It is my hope that Manding Medical Centre continues to be the template its today for generations to come. Let us learn from our mistakes and have the foresight and fortitude to turn them into something positive for all.

## After the Fall

Grandpa Bajoja advised that we have courage to accept our faults and fortitude to correct them for the good of all. The world is not always our making but we must make the best of it.

Mrs. Binta Ceesay (my elder sister)

# Dr. Alhasan Sisawo Ceesay, MD

# Chapter 8

## PRISONER OF MY AMBITION FOR THE VILLAGER

The burning embers of a wish and hope for my people became a prison wall that kept caving onto me any time I relaxed my effort. Ambition to bring the golden Flees, in the form of medical aid, to the villager constantly hunts me and reminds me of my covenant for the Gambia.

There were no doubts in my mind that I was rightfully engaged in bringing much needed medical service to the region served by Manding Medical Centre in the Gambia. I literally became the fugue of the family as I pushed to bring my desire to provide proper medical aid into fruition for the villager in the North Bank of the Gambia.

This quest for a better medical service to neglected villagers led to my disappearing from the family horizon to America as early as 1967. There I started the challenge of my life in a drive to become a doctor of medicine serving the Gambia.

The path of this adventure is well documented in my first book, "The legend against all odds" published by Publish America, Baltimore, Maryland, USA in August 2002.

## After The Fall

The strength of my conviction along with a mindset to do something concrete for my people made me give up today's pleasures for a better tomorrow for the Gambia. An Armchair psychologist, Dr. Kube Lonna (nick named Dr. Hamham), once told me. "Dreamers are a pain in the neck". I asked why?

And he replied, "They wake up with one of the most ridiculous ideas and try not only to live in that nonsense but implement them for the rest of their lives. Us pragmatics and wise become sceptical and weary of the dreamer and brand him either a total loony or living in a planet by himself or herself".

I replied quoting Lawrence of Arabia. Who said "All men dream: but not equally. Those who dream by the night In the dusty recesses of their minds wake in the day to find that it was vanity; but the dreamers of the day are dangerous men, for they act their dream with open eyes to make it possible."

I further made it clear that none the less many dreamers have converts. I asked what converts the sage to the dreamer' path? To this he gave the most amazing reply in favour of the dreamers and people with strong convictions like mine.

## Dr. Alhasan Sisawo Ceesay, MD

My armchair psychologist told me, "We only become flabbergasted as the dream unfolds to bits of reality opening up wide realms unknown to us before that day". He continued by illustrating what he meant. "Take for example the case of the Rights brothers and their attempt to fly.

Boy oh boy! Some critics who strongly believed that only birds, goblins, and angels had the privilege of flight ridiculed the Rights brothers as witches. Today you and I know better for we now use the Rights brother's dream to fly round the world at ease and by it we have catapulted to the moon and beyond".

I hope this has cleared the air for the reader as to why some of us are considered as whacks and a challenge to my friend the sage armchair psychologist Dr. Kube Lonna. Very early in my high school days friends labelled me as a reclusive person not knowing that my whole psyche was based on going aboard and becoming one of the future doctors of the Gambia.

I am fully aware of all work and no play not only turns us into monsters but also indeed a very dull one at that. I just moderated my life and made certain that I never lost track of my direction in life and my ambition for the Gambian villager.

## After The Fall

After ten years in America my family considered me being lost in zealous desire to gain book knowledge or Western education. I learnt that my father, while on his deathbed urged that prayers be offered so that I, the family fugue would return home.

Like Mac polo or Sinbad's adventures mine had seen me fly on several times to America, Liberia, the West Indies and the United Kingdom seeking more skills with which to serve my people.

It is said that life is lonely at the top but I found it even lonelier when struggling from ground zero with no hope of financial assistance at sight. Every hour of my life had to be organized in a way to minimize loss of income and to maintain progress in my academic pursuits. Hence I worked on three jobs during the summer breaks and at school libraries to raise funds for my education or repayment of loans which enable me continue schooling.

To me every ounce of energy and cent spent on my aspiration to become a doctor in the Gambia was as exhilarating as becoming an overnight multimillionaire. It is a joy I wish I could share with you. Graduating from medical school and my first patient in the Gambia are indelible blessed moments I hold dear to my heart. The rewards will forever be for my people and humanity.

Dr. Alhasan Sisawo Ceesay, MD

# Chapter 9

## DISTIGUISHED 2005 GRADUATE AWARD TO DR. ALHASAN CEESAY

I attended Alpena Community College (ACC) in Michigan, USA, from September 1967 to December 1979. My contact with friends at Alpena never waned. Hence the wheels of profound recognition by the institute started rolling when Mathew Dunckel called me to let me know he read my book, "The Legend against All Odds".

He was very impressed and intrigued by my experience and fortitude since my leaving Alpena Community College in 1979. I met Mathew when he was twelve years old. His father Dr. Elbridge Dunckle was my academic advisor while I was at Alpena community College.

I will without any reservation still recommend Dr. Dunckel for academic advisor to any foreign student attending the college.

It was during one of our telephone conversation (02/01/05) that Mathew told me of the possibility of ACC recommending me for the Distinguished 2005 Graduate award offered annually by Alpena Community College to its outstanding Alumni.

## After The Fall

Alpena Community College foundation recognizes its graduates annually for their academic and their career accomplishment for their communities. It simply recognizes the aspirations of Alumni for their people. The Pandora's Box was opened by innocuous telephone conversation in recognizing my aspiration and goal for providing medical aid to Gambian villagers.

Mathew asked me to fax him any and all possible documentation about me and work I do in the Gambia. He would then speak to the relevant authorities regarding my being nominated for the Distinguished 2005 graduate of Alpena Community College coming May $5^{th}$ 2005 spring/summer commencement. Mathew did just as promised. In a nutshell, here is the letter from Mrs. Penny Boldrey, Executive Director Alpena Community College Foundation. It read:-

Alpena Community College

666 Johnson Street

Alpena, MI 49707

January 6, 2005

Dr. Alhasan Sisawo Ceesay, MD

Alhasan S. Ceesay, MD

245 Great Western Street

Manchester M14 4LQ

England

Dear Dr. Ceesay,

Mathew Dunckel shared the information that you recently provided to him regarding your professional achievements since your early years at Alpena Community College. I'm extremely pleased to share with you that your many outstanding accomplishments have earned you the distinction of Distinguished Graduate of Alpena Community College (ACC) for 2005.

We commend you for your humanitarian efforts in founding and developing the Manding Medical Centre in Gambia, West Africa. I'm anxious to read your book. "The legend against all odds" once Matt has finished with it.

Without a doubt, you serve as an example of how a solid educational foundation from Alpena Community College can launch a lifetime of achievements. You will be honoured at our spring commencement exercises on Thursday, May 5, which begins at 7 pm, in the Park Arena at ACC.

## After The Fall

We invite you to join us on that evening. However, we certainly understand that making a trip to the United States, on so short a notice, may not be feasible. During the commencement program, I will share a synopsis of your extraordinary career that has earned you the honour of Distinguished Graduate.

If you are able to join us, you will be invited to join me at the podium to receive your award and to address the audience if you wish. Would you be willing to provide us with the following:

1) a copy of your professional resume;

2) a paragraph on your memories of ACC and how your experience helped you achieve your goals;

3) a professional photo for use in our alumni newsletter as well as in an ad that will appear in Alpena news. Please feel free to call me or e-mail me with any additional questions you may have. Again, congratulations! We look forward to hearing from you in the future.

Sincerely

Penny Boldrey

Executive Director

## Dr. Alhasan Sisawo Ceesay, MD

My response to this honour and invitation to my second home America was swift and obvious as penned bellow. I e-mailed Penny forth with as my heart was overwhelmed by joy for being recognised by my Alma Mata ACC. It simply stated:-

13/01/05,

Manchester, UK.

Dear Penny Boldrey,

I am overwhelmed and do not know where to begin this note of thanks to Alpena Community College. In my mind it's the American people who deserve such honour and distinction for I am only recipient of the goodness of the Americans. I am humbled and further rejuvenated by the thought and recognition of my goals and work for the Gambia.

I remember in the 60s when people used to tell me, "You will end up just like all foreign students who came to America. They end up getting trapped by the greener pasture syndrome of America."

To such challenges my response had always been; I for one will disappoint a lot of you for I will never rest until I bring to my people the American know how and willingness to share with others.

## After The Fall

This stance has never changed and will not ever change because the only way I can, in a small measure compared to what you did for us poor ones, pay back is to be able to show what the USA is all about and her stand for the little guy anywhere on this planet.

I will look into my schedule to see if I can afford to be in Alpena May 2005. I will let you know by the end of February 2005. Mean while I'm faxing a resume and will try to send my photos by e-mail.

Where it is not possible for me to attend in May, would it be okay for my first Alpena family friend, Mrs. Rita Riggs to represent me at the ACC' spring Commencement Ceremony. She was the first people in Alpena that opened their homes to me.

She and her family will certainly appreciate recognition of their help to this simple Gambian. None the less rest assured that I have not yet slammed the door to my seeing Alpena once more. Timing and visa problems might make it unattainable. Again, please accept profound gratitude to all of you and to Alpena Community College. God blesses you and rain peace on earth in 2005. Cheers and regards.

Sincerely

Dr. Alhasan S. Ceesay, MD

Dr. Alhasan Sisawo Ceesay, MD

My lovely daughter: Binta Ceesay

After The Fall

Mrs. Boldrey replied thus:

ACC, Michigan 49707

13/01/05

Hi Dr. Ceesay,

Yes, I did receive your curriculum vitae and thank you for forwarding that to me! We are extremely proud of you and your accomplishments! Once I get my hand on your book, I will pay special notice to the ACC chapter.

The best part of my job is the opportunity to meet former alumni and learn of the impact ACC had in their lives. Please believe me that we understand if you are unable to join us at commencement on May 5. Indeed we would be pleased to have Rita Riggs accept this honour on your behalf. Rita is remarkable and kind woman.

My husband speaks fondly of her and has stayed in close contact with her. I look forward to getting to know you better through our correspondences! And meet you in person someday. Regards

Its

Mrs. Penny Boldrey

Executive Director

## AFTER THE FALL

At the end it was not possible for me to attend the ceremony in person. So Rita Riggs and her family stepped in for me. Her elder son Robert Riggs was designated to receive the award in my behalf as representative of Rita who was in her 80s at the time.

I emailed the follow short remarks to be read by Robert Riggs at the time the award is given. It is titled:-

A FUTURE FOR ALL

Mr. President, staff, Graduates, Ladies and Gentlemen; I am deeply moved and humbled being chosen Alpena Community College's Distinguished Alumni for 2005.This recognition belongs to America.

Without the good will and foresight of the staff, students and the community of Alpena in 1967, I might never have had the chance to earn education with which to help my people move forward in life.

Dr. Alhasan Sisawo Ceesay, MD

Hence, allow me reiterate profound gratitude to Alpena Community College, my fellow students, people of Alpena and America at large. My life after Alpena has been full of trials and tribulations detailed in my first book, "The legend against all odds".

One relief in it is the robust blessing and peace of mind I have knowing that I am right in what I am doing for my people. There are those who claim Heaven in being rich but for me it is reaching out to help others that matters in life.

Upon graduating from medical school, I returned to the Gambia and setup a self-help village Health organization (Manding Medical Centre) at Njawara village in an effort to provide a much needed medical service to the rural sector. I am happy to report that membership has grown beyond twenty thousand villagers.

Please join me to catch a dream for my villagers. Manding medical centre will help portray the America we all dream of and yearn to be part. We are on the verge of building the children's unit and do need monetary, equipment and medicines assistance in our drive to provide this unique service to villagers.

## After The Fall

To the graduates, I would like to remind you that, the great tide of history flows and as it flows it carries to the shores of reality what binds us as one human race. Be aware of the extent, depth and gravity of the challenges ahead as you set out to transform, reconstruct and integrate America into a global icon.

Sincere congratulations for your march towards success and fulfilment. Alpena Community College has given you the first footprints. Walk your way with head held high and determination to succeed in the world. Confucius said, "Our greatest glory is never failing, but in rising every time we fail."

Stockpiles of atomic bombs or weapons of mass destruction and dictators do not measure greatness. I believe strongly and sincerely that with deep-rooted wisdom and dignity, innate respect for human right and lives, the intense humanity will make us more cherished and better leaders.

This will make us able to contribute towards the future and progress of mankind. I am happy for you and hope that you will fly the American flag for it is the great American constitution.

## Dr. Alhasan Sisawo Ceesay, MD

Finally, I would like to pay tribute to pass and present staff, students of ACC and Alpena community for having given me the opportunity to forge for my people. Allow me make special mention and express thanks to the remarkable and noble friends I met in Alpena.

Sincere thanks from my family, villagers and I to Howard & Rita Riggs, Judge Philip & Viola S. Glennie, Mr. Henry V. Valli, Dr. Elbridge Dunckel, Dr. Strom, Bill & Magritte Cruise, Dr. Charles T. Egli and the Alpena medical association, Mr. Cloyd Ramsey & the Medical Arts Clinic and all who helped make my sojourn to Alpena a remarkable success.

If I have a million friends, I would like many more to be like you. I hope you will believe in, as well as join me, in my dream of providing modern medical aid to the Gambian villagers. Thanks a million and God bless America!

BY: DR. ALHASAN SISAWO CEESAY, MD

Mrs. Penny Boldrey called to let me know she confirmed the details with Robert Rigg, who was selected by the family to deliver the speech.

After the Fall

She assured me that Bob was all set with my remarks and had been practicing many times. Rita and Donna will also be attending with other friends. To make it official she sent this note to Robert Riggs (Bob).

April 21, 2005


Robert Rigg

312 Liberty Street

Alpena, MI 49707


Dear Bob,

Dr. Alhasan Ceesay has informed that you will be representing him at our commencement ceremony and accepting the Distinguished Graduate Award on his behalf. Our spring commencement exercises will be held on Thursday, May 5, at 7 pm.

There will be VIP seating near the front left section of the Park Arena for and your family. During the commencement program, I will share a brief synopsis of Dr. Ceesay's career.

Dr. Alhasan Sisawo Ceesay, MD

I will invite you to join me at the podium to receive Dr. Ceesay's Distinguished Graduate Award. Following the presentation, you will have the opportunity to share Dr. Ceesay's remarks.

I shared with Dr. Ceesay that his comments must be kept brief (2-3 minutes) because our program consist of many individuals who will also be addressing the graduating class.

After the ceremony we would like to take some photographs, so if you could remain near your seats, I will come to you. A reception at the Jeese Besser Museum follows commencement and you are also invited to join. Enclosed you will find a copy of Dr. Ceesay's remarks.

I look forward to hearing from you. Please call me to confirm your participation.

Sincerely

Penny Boldrey

Executive Director

Two weeks prior to the ceremony I received an e-mail letting me know that Karen Eller, administrative assistant in the president's (ACC) office of Public information will be writing about me in the Lumberjack Link spring /summer alumni newsletter publication.

## After The Fall

Penny also told me that Kerrie Miller (also alumni) and news writer for The Alpena News would like to feature me in the local paper. I immediate e-mailed the following to Kerrie Miller at the Alpena News.

Hi Kerrie, I just received Penny's email with the good news that you want to feature me in the Alpena News. For me this would be a dream come true. Yes! By all means go ahead and feel free to contact me should you want more information about me or the work I'm doing in the Gambia.

I am a simple person that loves to help others get on with life the best way they can during their short sojourn on mother earth. I strongly believe that those of us who had the privilege to learn from America have responsibility to share American goodwill with our people.

That is the only way they, our people, can experience the real America that stands for the down trodden and the innovative. I still feel very happy when come across an American. If your paper is able to help me get Manding Medical Centre at Njawara out of its current limbo, then you would have participated in the most noble and worthy course that will outlive us and will be a spring board of hope and medical service for generations we can ever dream of.

Dr. Alhasan Sisawo Ceesay, MD

It is my Binta Ceesay, Brusubi, Gambia 2013

## After The Fall

We are still on fund raising stage to build the first phase, the children's unit, which according to estimates will cost around £250,000 or about $500,000 dollars. I committed all proceeds of my book, "The legend against all odds", to the centre but it is not selling enough to get things in fast gear. I need help to bring relief to my villagers.

Well, this is enough introductions until I hear from you. God bless you and thanks a million for being kind towards us.

Sincerely

Dr. Alhasan S. Ceesay

Kerrie Miller replied and asked that I send her a synopsis of how I found out Alpena in the 60s. So I sent her the following summary. "I came to be in Alpena by simply going to the then American Consulate in Banjul, the Gambia and asked for a catalogue with information on American colleges.

As a beggar normally has no choice, I started from the top alphabets. Well, Alpena Community college was there and was the first that accepted my application among the schools that replied to my desire to pursue further education in America.

## Dr. Alhasan Sisawo Ceesay, MD

This part is well expanded in chapter in my book "The legend against all odds" highlighting my experience at Alpena Community College from 1967 -1969. I was born and bred in abject poverty and I'm only fighting for my villagers to have a chance to proper medical care etc, etc nothing more and nothing -less. I hope you will help get your readers interested in Manding Medical Centre and its objective for the villagers.

Thank you for taking upon the task of writing about me and my work in the Gambia. Manding Medical Centre is in limbo and we year for a boost or a short in the arm to get things moving faster. Please visit our website: www.Friends of manding gambimed.com

It's

Dr. A. Ceesay

I will later reproduce both articles written by Karen Eller for the Lumberjack Link and Kerrie Miller's in the Alpena News respectively. For now let us head to the spring commencement podium and listen to what Mrs. Penny Boldrey has in mind about this simple village doctor.

Bob and his family attended in time and it was now time for Penny's remarks about my achievements from the days of Alpena Community College to now.

## After The Fall

It is simple and movingly started thus:-

"Good evening and congratulations graduates!

The Alpena Community College Foundation created the Distinguished Graduate award not only to recognize, but to honour our graduates who have gone on to contribute to society through successful careers.

Our recipient tonight serves as an example of how a solid education foundation from ACC can launch a lifetime of achievements.

I'm pleased to share with you that our 2005 Distinguished Graduate is Dr. Alhasan Ceesay from the Gambia, West Africa. Dr Ceesay received his Associates of Arts Degree in 1969, exactly two years after leaving the Gambia. He credits many individuals, and the generosity of others, as the driving force behind his success.

Following his graduation from ACC, Dr. Ceesay transferred to Olivet College, on a full-tuition scholarship provided to him by the Besser Foundation. In 1971, he earned a Bachelor of Arts Degree in Biology from Olivet, and in 1973 completed his Master of Science degree from Michigan Technological University at Houghton Michigan, USA.

## Dr. Alhasan Sisawo Ceesaay, MD

Dr. Ceesay taught biology for several years in the Gambia before entering into medical school in 1992, he was awarded his Doctor of Medicine Degree from the American University of the Caribbean.

Dr. Ceesay again returned to the Gambia, and provided free medical assistance to the villagers for an entire year before he took a position as House Officer at the Royal Victoria Hospital, Banjul, the Gambia, and was eventually promoted to the post of Medical Officer in 1999.

He is the proud founder of the Manding Medical Centre, a self-help village Health organisation located in the Gambia, which has provided much needed medical care to over 8000 villagers.

In his autobiography, "The legend Against All Odds", Dr. Ceesay shares his struggle to survive in his quest for an education. All the proceeds from his book go to supporting the Manding Medical Centre.

Dr. Ceesay and his wife have three daughters, ages 14, 11 and 7. In my correspondence with Dr. Ceesay over the past few months, he shared his profound gratitude for his American education.

## Dr. Alhasan Sisawo Ceesay, MD

He said, "In my mind, it is the American who deserved such honour and distinction, for I'm the recipient of the goodness of the Americans."

Due to travel difficulties, Dr. Ceesay is unable to be here tonight to accept this award. However he has asked his first American family, the Howard Riggs family to represent him.

At this time I'll ask Bob Riggs to join me at the podium to accept the award for Dr. Ceesay. Indeed, it is truly an honour to recognize Dr. Ceesay for his many accomplishments and humanitarian efforts. We congratulate him on earning the Distinction of Distinguished Graduate of Alpena Community College. – Penny Boldrey-

Robert Riggs eloquently delivered my remarks aimed at the graduates and residents of Alpena city. It was welcomed as I was later told by those who were able to e-mail me. Alpena city and ACC were very happy. This Distinguished Graduate award came thirty 36 odd years since I last visited Alpena, Michigan.

Mathew Dunckel sent me the following comments about the evening of the award.

## After The Fall

"Alhasan, your address was given at commencement. It was the portion of the evening that was enjoyed by most. Partly because it was delivered well and partly because of my father was mentioned. I think what you said was inspirational for our students and brought home the need for them to think internationally.

Tom Ray is making final preparation to depart for Gambia early next week. What a great adventure for the students. I am looking forward to hearing about it on their return. Thank you for helping make it happen.

Your friend

Matt.

I sent Penny Boldrey the following; "I received both the award and enclosures. Accept my deepest appreciation for the kind words spoken about me in your presentation speech during the spring graduation ceremony. Thank you very much for your kindness."

I suggested we pursue the possibility of twining Alpena with two villages in the Gambia. Dear reader, I hope your patience is not running out as you eagerly look forward to the publication for alumni and friends of Alpena Community College.

## Dr. Alhasan Sisawo Ceesay, MD

Karen Eller wrote to let me know that she was assigned to write a news article for the local paper announcing my receiving the Distinguished Graduate award.

She read my book, "The legend against all odds," to garner more information about me to help her on the matter at hand. She continued by letting me know that she found my story very interesting and she intend to do a good job at the article.

Here without further ado is Karen Eller's article about me. This idea unfolded to reality in the chapter on sister city proclamation.

THE LUMBERJACK LINK: ALPENA MICHIGAN

DR. CEESAY NAMED DISTINGUISHED GRADUATE

Dr. Alhasan Sisawo Ceesay of the Gambia, West Africa, was recognized with the Distinguished Graduate award at the ACC spring commencement ceremony in May $5^{th}$, 2005. On hand to receive the award for Dr. Ceesay was members of the Howard Riggs family, his first host family when he came to Alpena in 1967.

According to Dr. Ceesay, "The Riggs were the ideal American, an average working class who readily shared the little bit God gave them with others less fortunate."

## After The Fall

Dr. Ceesay earned his Associate of Arts degree from ACC in 1969 and went on to Olivet College to earn his Bachelor's degree in biology with the help of a full-tuition scholarship from the Besser Foundation. He earned his Master's degree in biological sciences from Michigan Technological University in 1973.

In 1979, Dr. Ceesay returned to Africa and entered the University of Liberia Medical School in Monrovia. Because of political unrest in the Gambia in 1981, Dr. Ceesay escaped to the United States in hopes of completing his lifelong dream; "to provide medical relief to the villager who is forced to walk miles on end to seek medical aid for his already dying child, wife or friend."

During the time he was seeking political asylum in the United States, Dr. Ceesay never gave up his quest for education, and he continued to take classes at Michigan State University and Wayne State University.

He was finally accepted at the American University of the Caribbean in the West Indies, and he began the final segment of his journey to becoming a doctor.

In 1992, after 25 years of educational struggles, Dr. Ceesay was awarded his Doctor of Medicine degree from the American University of the Caribbean.

Dr. Alhasan Sisawo Ceesay, MD

He returned to the Gambia where he provided free medical assistance to the villagers for an entire year before taking a position at the Royal Victoria Hospital, Banjul, The Gambia.

Dr. Ceesay founded Manding Medical Centre in 1993. This is a self-help village health organisation which provides much needed medical aid to the villagers of the Gambia, West Africa. His autobiography, "The legend against all odds," chronicles his struggle to survive in his quest for Western education.

Proceeds of his book go to support Manding Medical Centre at Njawara village and provide scholarships in medicine and agriculture for indigent rural candidates in the Gambia. To learn more about Dr. Ceesay's ambitions, you can e-mail him at alhasanceesay@hotmail.com.

Dr. Ceesay was honoured to receive this distinction from ACC and would like to "express thanks to the remarkable and noble friends" he met in Alpena. He credits the goodwill and foresight of the staff and students at ACC for giving him the chance to earn an education and help move his people forward in life.

-Karen Eller-

## After The Fall

I thank Karen Eller for this revealing commendable article. Here now is that featured by the Alpena News written by news staff Kerrie L. Miller. This is Miller's version about me and my goals.

ALPENA NEWS, MICHIGAN, USA 2005

A LONG ROAD FROM GAMBIA TO ALPENA

When he was about 14, Dr. Alhasan S. Ceesay saw a family tragedy unfold that would change his life forever.

As he was walking to school, he saw a woman, pregnancy full-term, who was obviously ill. Her husband was carrying their young son who was nearly comatose from illness.

Ceesay later found out the pregnant woman's baby died in uterus and she died from the toxins built up in her body as a result. The young boy also died three quarters of a mile before his family was able to reach the health centre at Kerewan village.

"That day I said, "If God will help me, no one will ever have to go through that again. That picture is what made up my mind for me," Ceesay said. Ceesay, a native of Njawara, Gambia, is a graduate of Alpena Community College, class of 1969.

## Dr. Alhasan Sisawo Ceesay, MD

He earned his Associate's of Arts degree from ACC before attending Olivet College, Michigan Tech and Howard University, earning his doctor of medicine degree from the America University of the Caribbean in 1992.

But how does a young man from a village in Gambia get to Alpena to attend its community college? In an e-mail message, he stated that after reaching the American Consulate, and asking for a listing of American colleges, Alpena Community College was at the top of the alphabetical list.

And Acc was the first to respond to his application. Once here, life was not without challenges. In a telephone conversation, he said it was the first time he had left his country, and when he got here no one spoke his language. "But I don't give up," he said.

Another goal Ceesay never gave up on was making it possible for village families, such as those like the one who affected him as deeply as a young man, to have access to health care services. With the creation of the Manding Medical Centre, which has helped over 8000 patients free of charge, he is doing that.

## After The Fall

Though progress has been very slow in coming to the centre; Ceesay said officially he is employed by the central government and is only on the weekends is he able to man the centre, along with three or four other doctors who volunteer their time. Ceeesay say the centre sees no fewer than 500 patients and as many as 1,500 patients in a weekend.

He said currently the centre is in limbo and is a little more than a shed. He has been working on fund-raising to get the first phase, a children's unit, built. It is expected to cost approximately $500,000.

Members of the ACC Leadership Class are currently conducting fund-raising to go to Gambia and help with the children and volunteering at the centre. The trip will last two weeks.

Ceesay is the author of a book chronicling his life's experiences called "The legend against all odds" (available at Amazon .com) and he has committed all proceeds of its sale to the centre.

He said he's never regretted the decision he made to become a doctor. "Sometimes I feel like I have oil on my feet and I'm climbing a very steep hill." Ceesay said.

## Dr. Alhasan Sisawo Ceesay, MD

"I have always believed I'll reach my goal... you have to be crazy like me and you have to ignore lots of things that take you away from your goals."

A typical day in Ceesay's life begins at 5 am with prayer, before boarding public transportation to the hospital where he works, 7 miles from his home. From 7 – 11 am he does morning rounds, followed by clinics, then evening rounds. Days can last up to 10 or 11 pm before he heads back home.

"In between, I try to please my wife and children. It's a very simple life really," he said. He and his wife have three daughters, the oldest of which has dreams of attending Alpena High School and ACC before going onto medical school like her father.

Ceesay's long-term goals revolve around the medical centre, which he hopes will continue to grow for generations, helping thousands more patients. "I plan to stay at the centre until the day they bury me. That and have my children educated. That's it," he said.

-Kerrie Miller-

## After The Fall

Kerrie sent me a copy of the Alpena news. And I sent the following in appreciation of the good work in the article. Kerrie, I just received a copy of the Alpena news featuring me. It was a job well done.

I hope it help move my dream of providing medical aid to villagers a notch higher for Manding Medical centre and the Gambian villagers. The Gambia and I are most grateful for enlightening your readers about us and our need for a medical facility.

Extend our thanks and deep appreciation to the staff and Alpena-news. We shall definitely be in Gambia in due course. We look forward to your crew attending the ground breaking ceremonies in Gambia soon.

I have started a collection of documentations about me to be placed in Dr. Alhasan S. Ceesay's achieves. Kerrie Miller replied saying that they missed me for the ceremony but she look forward to attending the grand opening of the centre.

Penny Boldrey simply said, "I will certainly make sure you receive a copy of our alumni newsletter once it's completed. Indeed, we are very proud of your accomplishments and humanitarian efforts."

Dr. Alhasan Sisawo Ceesay, MD

Chapter 10

AMERICAN GUESTS VISIT MANDING MEDICAL CENTR,

NJAWARA, THE GAMBIA, IN MAY 2005.

The telephone call on 5/01/05 from Mr. Mathew Dunckel as well as that from Mr. Thomas Ray (TOM) four days later opened the Pandora's box and became harbingers to a remarkable trip to Manding Medical Centre, Njawara village, Gambia by the Alpena Community College's Leadership class headed by none other than their instructor Mr. Thomas P. Ray.

I contacted Mr. Thomas Ray as soon as it was brought to my attention that some ACC students were contemplating visiting my centre at Njawara in May 2005. My message on the 6/01/05 to Mr. Ray ran thus:-

"An old friend, Mr. Mathew, staff of ACC, had a long chat with me last night and he brought to my attention of a possibility that a class wanting to travel to the Gambia as guest of Manding Medical Centre at Njaswara. I am more than willing and happy to pave the way for those that would venture the trip.

## After The Fall

I do need an e-mail or fax from you indicating desire to go to the Gambia on a mission for Manding Medical Centre. I will speak to both the schools and the district authority about your most welcomed trip to the Gambia.

Manding Medical Centre is a self-help village health organisation I setup in upon returning to the Gambia in1992. We provide medical service to villagers and land has been donated for the location of the centre and its ancillaries. We only have a corrugated shed as clinic.

We are now on the verge of building the first phase, being the children's unit of the centre and need monetary assistance. I am delighted to know of your intentions. Please contact me as soon as you speak with the class."

Thomas Ray replied on 7/01/05, "I was thrilled when Mathew discussed the possibility of a trip to Gambia for our leadership students. I will meet with the whole class next week to discuss the possibility.

As I am sure you are aware the cost of airfares from Alpena to Gambia is high, so I will need to be certain the students are committed to raising the money needed before we begin making plans.

Dr. Alhasan Sisawo Ceesay, MD

I have travelled to many locations, but never to Africa, so I am also very excited about the prospects for myself. After I meet with the students on Tuesday of next week, I will e-mail you with further information.

I wish to also commend you for your personal achievements; I plan to purchase a copy of your recent book to share with my students and for my personal reading. Thank you for your help and enthusiasm."

I emailed Tom advising that to bargain for insured group tickets. Tom further contacted me on 12/01/05 stating that he has spoken to the students and they have agreed to take on a service trip as part of the course.

He told me that they would only be able to travel in a group for 10 – 14 days in May 2005. Tom wanted to know if there was an existing program at Njawara that would be able to accommodate the students.

He assured me that the students would be comfortable in a dormitory housing or make shift dormitories. In addition I let him know on the 14/01/05 that I have spoken to the commissioner, North Bank Division and the local authority in Lower Badibou district regarding their pending trip to Njawara as guest of Manding Medical Centre and the region.

## After The Fall

I assured him that these authorities would be more than happy to have his class visit with them. I requested an e-mail from him stating that they are visiting in behalf of Manding Medical Centre at Njawara and specify what they would want to do while in the Gambia. I suggested that they can help teach in some of the schools.

I assured them that even though business and some residents have moved out there is still some activity at the village. Tom in reply sent the following on the 15/01/05. "Thank you for the great news. I am very excited about the prospect and have begun searching for group airfares with special student rates.

I will inform the students on Tuesday and contact you immediately afterward via email. I have a few questions. What costs do we need to expect in Gambia and in your village? How will we travel from Banjul to the village?

We need to be certain we have a clear idea what expenses we will have to help us set specific fundraising goals both for ourselves and for the foundation from which we hope to receive grants.

When I write the other e-mail, are there tasks other than tutoring that I should include? Are there other ways we can help while we are there?

Dr. Alhasan Sisawo Ceesay, MD

I am more excited about the prospect of this service trip everyday and the students are quite enthused." In another e-mail dated 15/02/05, Tom wrote, "The students in the leadership class are so committed to this project that they voted to contribute their own money toward the travel if they cannot raise enough.

This means that the number of students who actually travel will likely be fewer, but that we will be able to travel to Njawara in May. I have begun drafting the letter to the commissioner many times, but I have some questions. Am I asking the commissioner to help organise local housing for us?

Do I want his permission to visit Njawara? Should I tell him what we would like to do there? What subject might they tutor? Are there any construction projects for the centre or the village with which we could help?

I would also like to know if there are any material supplies we could bring with us to donate to the centre or the village. One possible way for us to save money would be to fly into Dakar, Senegal and travel from there overland to Njawara. All the above concerns and questions were answered but a small hiccup in fundraising occurred leaving a distinct possibility that the students will not be able to raise enough to make the trip.

## After The Fall

The reason being the major source of funding for the trip fell through. This left all of us jittery but Tom and his students were in no mood to change their plans to travel to the Gambia in May 2005.

On the same day 15/02/05 I received the following from Mr. Jay Walterriet, Director of Public information for Alpena Community College. It stated that he was asked to contact me for more photos of myself and the clinic at Njawara.

He wanted more information regarding the Leadership planned trip to Gambia. I was told that the local television station would like to do a segment on the Leadership class and their trip. As part of the segment photos were needed.

I sent all photos that were relevant to enable the reporter to do his TV-segment on the planned Leadership trip to Njaswara, Gambia. Mr. Jay on the 17/02/05 emailed thanking me for providing the requested photos and assured me that ACC has received good deal of interest from the local media regarding the Leadership class trip and both he and Penny Boldrey were trying to provide all of the information they could.

My e-mail was given to reporters who might want to contact me for more information.

Dr. Alhasan Sisawo Ceesay, MD

The entire twenty students could not enlist for the final take off to Africa. So Thomas Ray and 11 students took on the venture of their life time to the Gambia as guest of Manding Medical Centre at Njawara village.

On 17 February 2005 Tom sent me a copy of the final letter he sent to the commissioner and the local authority at the Lower Badibou district spelling out their intentions and wish while guests of the Manding Medical Centre for a two weeks duration. Here it is.

Thamos P. Ray

Alpena Community College

666 Johnson Street

Alpena, Michigan 49707

17 February 2005


Dear Commissioner Batala Juwara,

I am pleased to inform you of our plans to visit Njawara on behalf of the Manding Medical Centre. I am the advisor and instructor for a group of college students from Alpena Community College in Michigan in the USA.

## After The Fall

We plan to visit Njawara in May and hope you will help us find lodging with local families during our stay. Our plan as of now is to fly out of the US on May $6^{th}$ to Banjul via London and to return on May $19^{th}$ 2005.

During our stay in Gambia, our hope is to provide any assistance we can to the community on behalf of the Manding Medical Centre. We would like to visit the school in Njawara and tutor the children and share stories and activities with them.

I also hope that we will have the opportunity to visit the important centres of the community and learn as much as we can in our short stay about the people and life in Njawara and Gambia.

I have communicated our plans with Dr. Alhasan Ceesay, who has kindly extended the invitation to us on behalf of the Manding Medical Centre.

Sincerely

Thomas P. Ray

English Instructor

Dr. Alhasan Sisawo Ceesay, MD

This letter was acknowledged by the commissioner and the district authority in the Gambia. Now that I was certain of the trip I set to inform my board members in like manner. The certainty of the trip was concretized by the following sent by Tom on 10 March 2005.

It simply updated me on the progress made regarding the trip; that the students have raised half the money needed to travel to Gambia. He affirms the fact that everyone concerned is working hard on the remaining sum. The arranged inoculations and are preparing to apply for visas to Gambia.

He said they were all enthused and has used my address in Gambia for the visa information requirement. Again, I was delighted for things are now heading the right direction for the historic and unique trip to Njawara.

I am now certain that more doors to boost ours and the centre's goals for the Gambia will be open by this simple friendly act of ACC. Here finally is my despatch the board members of Manding Medical Centre at Njawara village.

MANDING MEDICAL CENTRE/NJAWARA

UNITED KINGDOM CONTACT

After The Fall

245 GREAT WESTERN STREET

MANCHESTER, M14 4LQ

ENGLAND

E-MAI:alhasanceesay@hotmail.com

Tel/Fax: 44+161-342-0854

Date: 25/03/05

DEAR BOARD MEMBER,

I am pleased to bring to your attention about American guests to Manding Medical Centre at Njawara. Mr. Thomas Ray along with 11 Alpena Community college students will be visiting the Gambia as our guest in May 2005. They will be leaving the USA for the Gambia on May 6$^{th}$, 2005 and depart for United States on the 19$^{th}$, of May.

I would be most grateful if you give some of your time to meet them and make their visit memorable. There are many benefits to be accrued for the centre and the Gambia. I am at present arranging in the form of scholarships or placements in various fields of study at my previous college in Alpena Michigan.

Dr. Alhasan Sisawo Ceesay, MD

I have been in constant contact with Commissioner Batala Juwara at Kerewan and I would like all of you to brain storm and make this an ongoing link between us and Alpena Community College and other Michigan cities I am now in negotiation with. Alpena city has developed interest in our project.

I am also happy to report that my former college, Alpena Community College has awarded me, "Distinguished 2005 Graduate." Find enclosed correspondence from Mr. Thomas Ray, in behalf of the Leadership class of Alpena Community College, to Commissioner Juwara and Sefo Fafanding Kinte.

I look forward to your understanding and participation to help open up the Pandoa's Box of goodwill for the Gambia. This is a onetime opportunity for the Gambia that would make our two people linked for good goals and noble courses for generations of Gambians.

My regards and keep in touch.

Yours truly,

Dr. Alhasan S. Ceesay, MD

Founder/co-coordinator

Cc: Mr. Ousainu Darboe

## After The Fall

Mr. Fafa E. Mbai

Dr. Dawda Ceesay

Dr. Ayo Palmer

Mr. Saim Kinte

Mr. Sambou Kinte

Mr. Mustapha Njie

Mr. Maja Sonk

Mr. Dodou Ceesay

Mr. Sisawo Ceesay

Mrs. Mbee Sonko

On April 7$^{th}$ 2005, Tom updated me stating that the visa applications were going well and that most of the students have received their visas.

In addition let me privilege you the reader with some of the reactions emailed to me about the pending trip and what it would mean to them.

Alison Jane Smolensk said: "Hello Dr. Ceesay. I am one of the students in the Leadership class at Alpena Community College. I am really excited about the service trip, only a couple more weeks.

Dr. Alhasan Sisawo Ceesay, MD

Right now we are trying to prepare for the trip, just getting the basic necessities and what we should be packing. I just read about how you are building a bakery at Njawara. Even though our resources are limited, is there something we could do to help out? I thought we could help in some way.

I also just wanted to say thank you for the wonderful experience you giving to us. I realize it will be truly an eye opener. I feel as if I could never be able to repay you for these two weeks that you about to give us.

Thank you Dr. Ceesay!" Another email from Brittany Postumus simply stated; "I am one of the students from Alpena Community College that will be coming this May to help.

After learning all the things that you have done I must say you are an inspiration and the world can use more people who care as much as you do. I can't wait to come to Njawara. I am very excited to be able to help and thank you for the invitation."

Lastly, Ms. Grace Schmitz sent in the following before leaving for the Gambia. "I am a member of the Alpena Community College class that will be assisting you this May at Njawara. I am greatly looking forward to my visit to the Gambia.

## After The Fall

Thank you so much for the invitation! The Friends of Manding, a charitable Trust at Colchester had the following in its web site about the trip to Njawara, the Gambia. It read as "News flash 12 American visiting:"

"A class of 11 students and their instructor Mr. Thomas Ray from Alpena Community College, Alpena Michigan, will be visiting the Gambia as guest of Manding Medical Centre from the $6^{th}$ to $19^{th}$ May 2005. They will be visiting communities and tutor at local schools.

Alpena has developed interest in project Manding Medical Centre at Njawara. We are negotiating to have this exchange as an ongoing affair between Alpena and Njawara."

As time drew near to the flight to the Gambia Tom contacted the Commissioner on several occasions to clear last possible huddles that may surface. None the less preparations went smoothly and Thomas Ray and his ACC Leadership class left America on May $10^{th}$ 2005 via Madrid and then Dakar, Senegal before embanking at Banjul, the Gambia.

As fate would have the team instead hired a bus from Dakar to Hamdali village in the North Bank which was nearer to Njawara. I learnt they were given a VIP escort from Hamdali via Kerewan to Njawara village.

Dr. Alhasan Sisawo Ceesay, MD

As expected, I called the Mayor of Njawara, Mrs. Hadi Panneh enquiring about the American visitors. She told me they were fine and housed at the village centre, a semi motel used for foreign guest to Njawara. Tom and I spoke at length along with Sefo Fafanding Kinte.

Sefo Fafanding reassured me that everything possible will be done to help make "our guest comfortable and like wise a memorable visit in due course. I spoke briefly to the commissioner the next day to get a feedback from him.

The two week flew fast for the students most of who did want to leave at the time for kindness rendered by the villagers. It is said that good thing never last long and this the experience of the student who went to Njawara in May 2005. Here is the reaction of Americans after the trip to the Gambia.

The ACC students started sending their report and experience as guest of Manding Medical Centre, Njawara, The Gambia. Starting with Alison Jane Smolensk reported as bellow.

"Hello Dr. Ceesay: The trip to Njawara was incredible! I did not want to leave. It was an experience of a lifetime that I will never forget. Everyone in the village was very kind and helpful.

## After The Fall

I have never met such kind people in my entire life. I found the villagers doing everything possible to make their lives better. I realized that many people work together to get a job done or finished. This is absolutely wonderful.

Everyone was so helpful in the village. The people of Njawara gave us such wonderful hospitality. The food and shelter was more than we deserved. Also your wife, Mrs Fatou Koma-Ceesay, was all too good to us. We had a remarkable time with her at Bundung/Serekunda. Her cooking was excellent. And the gifts she gave all of us, we did not deserve.

Your family is wonderful and was too kind to us. I would like to thank you for the incredible experience you have given me. I could not have asked for anything more. I immensely enjoyed myself. I want to go back one day. I also want you to know that I will do my best to help in whatever way I can. I realize that action are louder than words and hope I can prove that to everyone. Thank you Dr. Ceesay."

Another reaction came from Grace Schiminitz. "I really enjoyed my time in Njawara. The people treated us very well and it was a pleasure to spend two weeks with them.

Dr. Alhasan Sisawo Ceesay, MD

Your wife is a wonderful person and was very hospitable to us. I will always be grateful for her kind treatment. I hope to make another visit to Njawara in the future. It is a wonderful place. It was an eye-opening experience. The people were absolutely marvellous.

They treated us as their own family and welcomed us with open hands. I had no idea that they would be that hospitable. I really miss walking to the river and spending time with the children. It was my first experience in Gambia and hopefully it will not be my last. I hope I can return their kindness.

I would love to see how the kids have grown up."The last but not the least came from Mr. Thomas P. Ray, English instructor at ACC. It read; "I want to thank you for the opportunity you provided my students on this trip. The entire experience was enjoyable and valuable as a means of teaching my students something about the responsibility that comes with the privileges they enjoy here.

Everyone was kind to us on the trip and the students came away with many great souvenirs and memories. I have many digital photos and am working on producing a CD of them to send out.

## After The Fall

I also plan to type up a version of my journal for posting on the internet and I will send parts of that to you. I plan to call the village this weekend to extend my appreciation to everyone.

Do you know anything about the proposed potential sister city relationship between Alpena and Njawara? I would like to start making some local contacts here to help that process. I am also hopeful that future trips will be possible for my students.

-Mr. Thomas P. Ray-

As you know very well man proposes but God dispose things. Tom took over the running of the department and with that came a hand full challenging responsibilities. He was not able to provide the CD until 11<sup>th</sup> of October 2005 after several reminders from me and those visiting my Website (www.friendsofmandinggambimed.btck.co.uk).

Finally, Tom contacted me on 4/11/05 to let me know he had the college mailing office send the CD of photos and other material registered delivery to me.

Then he made donation of $1000(one thousand us dollars) in the name of Friends of Manding, a Charitable Trust at Colchester Essex organising fund raising activities for Manding Medical Centre at Njawara the Gambia, West Africa.

Dr. Alhasan Sisawo Ceesay, MD

This cheque was duly received and forward registered mail to the Secretary of the Friends of Manding for depositing into our account at LLyod's Bank in Colchester Essex County. Tom asked about the state of the proposed sister-city program between Alpena and Njawara. Yes, this was one of my goals for inviting the Americans to my village in the Gambia.

I just believe that unveiling the false masks and stigma others have about Africa will create harmony in its unique way. People need to accept differences in the cultures. I transmitted all reactions presented by our American visitor to the Commissioner, the chief, and the village heads especially Hadi Panneh of Njawara village.

ALPENA: THANKS FOR TWINING WITH US/SISTER-CITY PROCLAMATION.

Having now been recognised as Distinguished 2005 Graduate by Alpena Community College I made a proposal for a twining relationship or sister-city status between Alpena and select villages in the Gambia. I, you guessed right, contacted Mathew Dunckel as a sound board or trial balloon for the above idea.

He replied that it was a sound idea and suggested my contacting the Alpena City Council members on the subject. He gave their web site thus:

## After The Fall

http://www.alpena.mi.us/council/members. In addition he gave the names of Councilman Dave Karschnik and Councilwoman Carol Shafto for me to initiate direct contact with the Alpena City Council. He told me that the mayor was John Gilmet and the City manager was Mr. Alan Bakalarski.

Armed with all this information and more I made my first push through Mrs. Penny Boldrey, Executive Director at Alpena Community College. I had no doubt if I get her interest in this unique wish she would do all within her power to not only contact the right people to make it eventually happen but would open up more doors for my villagers and our health project at Njawara.

Penny Boldrey upon hearing from mc linked with Councilwoman Shafto on the June 14th, 2005 thus; "Hi Carol, from one Distinguished Grad to another..... I received the enclosed message from our 2005 Distinguished Graduate, Dr. Alhasan Ceesay.

I' m wondering if perhaps you can help me with his inquiry regarding the possibility of twining between Alpena City and two villages in the Gambia, West Africa."

Dr. Alhasan Sisawo Ceesay, MD

Penny in turn informed me that she had contacted a good friend, Carol Shafto, who is a member of Alpena's City Council and also an Alpena Community College Distinguished 2003 Graduate, regarding my request for twining between the above communities. She enclosed Councilwoman Shafto's response to the idea.

My reaction was swift and my message to Councilwoman Carol Shafto ran thus:-"Hello Councilwoman Carol. Mrs Penny Boldrey sent me correspondence she had with you regarding a proposal I made to the city of Alpena.

My initial e-mail kick starting a twining proposal between the city of Alpena; Njawara and Kinte Kunda villages in the Gambia West Africa was sent to Mayor John F. Gilmet, Dave R. Karsctunick, Mike Polluch, Sam Eller and Carol Shafto.

It read, "I'm pleased to write and inform you that I am deputized by village heads of Njawara and Kinte Kunda to contact you and initiate a twining/sister city status proposal between Alpena and the above two villages. Njawara is my home village and Kinte Kunda is where I attended primary school in the early fifties.

## After The Fall

Tom Ray and the Leadership students visited both places during their two weeks stay in the Gambia. They met the chief of the district, Sefo Fafanding Kinte, at Kinte Kunda. Kinte Kunda has been the seat of many chiefs of the region and Fafanding is the most recent of several from this village.

Njawara is historically a trading centre connecting Gambia and the Northern part of Senegal. Today she has become a tourist destination. One can easily log onto information about Njawara village on the internet.

It boasts of lots of female education oriented projects. In addition it has an agricultural training centre."The contact was made in behalf of the village heads of the above and the local authority at the North Bank division of the Gambia.

This twining would be a very rewarding interaction and educational for both yours and the villagers. The people are eager to make worthwhile friendship with America. The chiefs and village heads have urged me to initiate their wish for the twining between them and Alpena or any city willing to go into such relationship with the villages.

Dr. Alhasan Sisawo Ceesay, MD

You can link up with Mr. Thomas Ray and his students for feedback on their experience as guests of Manding Medical Centre at Njawara village, the Gambia. The villagers and I would be most grateful if given the chance to link up with Alpena City.

Carol Shafto sent in this hiccup. "Dr. Ceeasy, I cannot proceed with any more discussions with the City Council of the City of Alpena until I am much clearer about what a Twining proposal entails. Could you please describe to me what you have in mind?

Although we may be supportive of your work at Njawara and Kinte Kunda in the Gambia; we cannot really act on your request until we know what we are agreeing to. Could you send me a brief outline of what you are seeking from the City of Alpena?

I will be happy to act as a liaison between you and the City, but cannot do so until I have a clear idea of what I am advocating for. Thank you most sincerely."

Carol Shafto

On July 13, 2005 I sent the required clarification to Councilwoman Carol Shafto as follows. Hello Carol, I am glad to hear from you.

## After The Fall

To be simplistically clear, twining means a sisterhood relationship between two cities for the mutual rewards of those involved. Hence it is a friendship like affair where people from Alpena can be part of and likewise the villages involved but at no cost to either party.

For example Councilwoman Shafto can choose to spend two weeks in Gambia helping reorganize or create a more functional administrative system or even learn from the villagers. In brief it is a two way international relationship. Or cultural dance -troupes from the Gambia villages can be coming to entertain Alpena, possibly more cities, during the summers.

This will help raise funds for the city, the villages, like wise for our health project at Njawara. It will provide much awareness and understanding of the two people merged in friendship. It is like adopting each other and opening up rewarding human adventures at no cost involved. In a nut-shell, it means ratified friendship between Alpena and the two villages.

I hope this makes it palatable for Alpena to want to be part of such endearing relationship. I thank you in behalf of the Kerewan local authority, the villagers and Commissioner for North Bank Division, the Gambia. God blesses all of you." Dr. Ceesay-

Dr. Alhasan Sisawo Ceesay, MD

Needless to say Councilwoman Carol Shafto was very pleased with the above clarification and appealed to Alpena City Council to consider the idea of twining in behalf of the Gambian villages.

Hence, Carol on the 13/7/05 sent me this e-mail following the receipt of the above message to the councilwoman. It simply states that, "I have forwarded this information to the mayor and city manager and offered to be the liaison if the City should consent to comply with this request. I will keep you posted with any development."

I updated the Commissioner and all concern at the Lower Badibou district regarding progress of my initiative with Alpena City few weeks after hearing from Councilwoman Carol Shafto. The Commissioner and the local authority sent me the bellow covering letter in support of my push for a twining relationship with Alpena City Michigan, USA. Njawara/Kinte Kunda

Lower Badibou District

North Bank Division

The Gambia, W. Africa

E-mail:njawaranato@yahoo.co.uk

After The Fall

November 5$^{th}$, 2005

To: Dr. Alhasan Ceesay

Manchester, England

Subject: Twining of Njawara, Kinte Kunda & Alpena Michigan

Dear Dr. Ceesay,

Your first letter dated September 23$^{rd}$, 2005 has been received and the content of which is understood, both the Commissioner, the Chief and the Alkalos (village heads) of Njawara and Kinte Kunda are very much interested in having Njawara, Kinte Kunda and Alpena City twined.

The Communities of both villages met and discussed the issue and they are very much happy about the lofty ideas. Njawara and Kinte Kunda are located in the Northern part of the Gambia. They are just about 60 kilometres away from the capital City Banjul, the Gambia.

Kinte Kunda is just 2 kilometres away from our administrative headquarters Kerewan where both the Commissioner and Area Council stay. Whereas Njawara ; is located 9 kilometres away from Kerewan. Regards

Dr. Alhasan Sisawo Ceesay, MD

Sincerely

Aja Hadi Panneh (Alkalo)

Alh. Fafanding Kinte (Chief Lower Badibou)

Cc: Mr. Batala Juwara (Commisioner NBD)

I replied to the above support with this note despatched immediately to the village Akalos, the Chief and Commissioner North Bank Division at Kerewan village.

245 Great Western Street

Manchester M14 4LQ

England

16/11/05

A BIG THANK YOU TO ALL

Dear Commissioner,

I'm profoundly grateful to you, Sefo Fafanding, the local authority (area Council and chiefs) and especially Alkalo Arfang Bah and people of Toro. Lastly but not the least a big thank you goes to the people of Badibou, Njawara and my sister Hadi Panneh Alkalo of Njawara village. I am very happy for support and understanding given to Manding Medical Centre.

## After The Fall

I'm pleased to inform you that I have initiated a twining process between Alpena and the villages of Njawara and Kinte Kunda. I have forwarded your note of 5/11/05 to the Alpena City Council. Copies were also sent to Mr. Thom Ray and the college.

Again, thank you for making our American friends happy and welcomed to our beloved country. God bless all of you. I will continue working for our development.

Sincerely

Dr. Alhasan S. Ceesay, MD

Director/Founder

Manding Medical Centre.

I then sent Carol Shafto the letter from the district authority plus this note urging action from her end.

245 Great Western Street

Manchester M14 4LQ

England

8/11/05

Dr. Alhasan Sisawo Ceesay, MD

Mrs. Carol Shafto

Councilwoman

Alpena City Council

208 North First Avenue

Alpena, MI 49707

Dear Mrs. Carol Shafto,

The enclosed is reply to your last e-mail dated 25/9/05 regarding the twining proposal made to the Alpena City Council earlier on in behalf of Njawara village and Kinte Kunda, the Gambia, respectively. The enthusiasm about having this relationship with Alpena is immeasurable. The villagers are looking forward to a warm and fruitful relationship between the two people. They all pray that you would be as eager to consummate it as they have already done in their wishes and hearts. Finally, may friendship and human kindness be an everlasting link between all humans. God bless you and we look forward for a positive reply soon. My personal regards and thanks to the City Council and all of Alpena.

Yours Sincerely

Dr. Alhasan S. Ceesay, MD

## After The Fall

It was not until September21, 2005 that I sent Councilwoman Shafto the following reminder and follow up note. "Hi Carol, I hope you had an enjoyable summer. This is a follow up of that lofty idea of twining Alpena City with Njawara and Kinte Kunda villages in the Gambia.

Has there been any movement forward at the Mayor's Office about the proposal made to the city? Is there anything I or the district authority in Gambia need do to bring this to fruition?

I have not heard anything about it since your last email of 14/7/05. Again, regards and thanks. I bank on your continued interest. God Bless."

–Dr. Ceesay-

The next day God smiled onto our dream to befriend America. Councilwoman Mrs. Carol Shafto sent me the following reply to the inquiry about the status of my dream for America and the Gambia.

It rang in the most melodious and cherished message I ever had for a long, long time after my being admitted into medical school and upon treating my first patient in the villages.

## Dr. Alhasan Sisawo Ceesay, MD

Here is Carol's email to me. "Good morning Dr. Ceesay: I appreciate your persistence in accomplishing this goal. Without that it surely would have failed. I do apologize for this delay. I have just returned this week from a wonderful month long tour of the UK and Ireland.

My last communication, before I left, with the City Manager was that this was a good idea, will be good for public relations, and that we should go forward with the proposal. The Mayor is also in favour. So there is absolutely nothing standing in the way of this happening. I am willing to do the work of it, but I honestly have no idea what to do.

Do you know procedures or paper work or any such thing from your end? Is it as simple as a proclamation? I would like to have more information about your village, your people, and why you are interested in twining with Alpena – what connection there is.

I would then put together a presentation for the City Council and ask them to decide that we are sister-cities (the term used here, although I know the UK and Europe use "twining) with the villages of Njawara and Kinte Kunda.

## After The Fall

We could erect a sign at the City entrance, etc. If you have any idea or directions for me, please let me know. Also any information you can provide on your village would be helpful. I will continue to work with you on this until it is accomplished.

Your friend in Alpena –

Carol Shafto

This was followed by my forwarding the bellow addendum to whatever had reached the Councilwoman's desk. Being the architect of this union much was expected from me.

And so I never relented supplying as much information as many times as I can afford. My phone bill sprouted to a Warping £600 etc. Most important was this addendum bellow.

SYNAPSIES OF NJAWARA/KINTE KUNDA VILLAGES

Njawara is a 350 years old market village situated on the bank of the Miniminiyang bolong, a creek of the River Gambia, in the Lower Badibou District of the North Bank Division of the Gambia. Njawara has a population of a thousand residents and is 95 kilometres from Banjul, Gambia's capital City.

Dr. Alhasan Sisawo Ceesay, MD

The village lies close to the Senegalese border and has been the trade links between Gambia and Senegal during the colonial days. Njawara was established and founded by the Panneh family of the Wolof tribe and initially called "Panneh village". The elderly still fondly refer to her as Mpanneh.

Among the residents of now Njawara are Mandingkas, Fulas, Sereres, Jolas, Konyanginkas, and Mabara tribes. All of whom are farmers, with few serving as petty traders, growing Peanuts, Rice, Coos, and a variety of vegetables.

The nearest government administrative post is 9 kilometres away at Kerewan village. Njawara lacked modern luxuries of electricity, proper telephones, sewer system, pave roads but water is now pumped from a nearby borehole.

The village has a thriving school and a dynamic citizenry working hard to improve their lot and the future of the younger generation.

KINTE KUNDA village has been the political base of Lower Badibou District for decades. It has provided us with several chiefs in the past and Sefo Fafanding Kinte is the most recent contribution. Kinte Kunda village comprises of mostly Mandinka tribes men and women.

## After The Fall

It is the home of venerable late Sefo Njako Kinte who, in the 30s ruled the district with an iron fist. It was he who imposed one of his brothers, Almami Kinte, to take over the administration or village headship of then Njawara(Mpanneh). None the less he was a respected chief.

Kinte Kunda was the first village that had a school in the entire Lower Badibou district and I am told that he chief insisted that the school be built in his home village leaving a row that lasted through his rein.

The village is now a smaller population than Njawara and the current appointed chief of the district, Sefo Fafanding Kinte resides there. Residents of Kinte Kunda are all farmers eager to improve their lives and those of their children.

They are friendly, peaceful, charming, descent hard working people who contributed a lot to growth of the Lower Badibou District in the North Bank. These two villages along with the entire Lower Badibou District yearn for this twining/sister-city status to come to realty. Hence, I enclose relevant messages regarding the proposed twining from the district authority as per fax from the Gambia.

Dr. Alhasan Sisawo Ceesay, MD

The villagers and I are interested in twining with Alpena Michigan n an effort to open up the Pandora's box of friendship, goodwill and more understanding of the people and cultures that would allow us relate in this shrinking globe we all share.

There is a lot we can do for each other once the ugly veil of ignorance, misunderstanding and fear is removed. And this can be done only learning and interacting with one another. I am sure the students, who went to the villages, can tell how much warmth and friendship they received from the villagers they met.

Exchange visits and whole host of beneficial programs to both parties can be organized within the framework of this twining. Once again, I personally appeal to the Mayor and City Council of Alpena to give this desire of the villagers a chance of fruition for Alpena City and the above villages in the Gambia.

BY: DR. ALHASAN SISAWO CEESAY, MD

In short while, I received the following reply from Councilwoman Carol Shafto of Alpena City Council letting me know of the final details, date of the be proclamation for the sister-city relationship between our villages and Alpena Michigan. Without further ado I present the message as sent on the 17$^{th}$ of November 2005.

# After The Fall

"Good Morning Dr. Ceesay

After many months of communication with you, I can finally announce a DATE for our Twining/Sister City Resolution! The Alpena City Council will adopt a resolution to establish a Sister City Program with Njawara/ Kinte Kinda on December 5$^{th}$, 2005.

I am going to be personally preparing the resolution. Since it will be a part of permanent records for both the villages and the City of Alpena, I would like be sure all of the information is accurate. Penny Boldrey suggested that I email the text to you after I complete it.

If you are willing, you could read it for any factual errors or omissions before I send it on to the City. If you are willing, I will send that via email when it is ready, sometime next week.

Meanwhile I am meeting with Tom Ray from the college who led the Leadership Class expedition to the villages. He is VERY enthusiastic about this proposal and is going to give me information and even share some pictures. We will be meeting next week.

Finally, I have invited several people to come to the City Council meeting to provide testimony and support for this proposal. Both Penny Boldrey and Tom Ray will be there.

Dr. Alhasan Sisawop Ceesay, MD

Also they are inviting some of the students who went to the villages to also be present and speak to the issue. So it would be a very nice presentation and will be more than just a formality.

Also, if you would like, I can arrange to have a tape of the meeting sent to you. Our meetings are videotaped and played for the public on the public access television channel several times a week, between meetings. I can make a copy of the tape of the meeting and have it send you or to the village officials or both if you would like.

Also, the resolution will have an official seal of the City of Alpena and the signature of the Mayor. I will have as many copies as you need made and will laminate them so they will be preserved. I will send those to you and/ or whomever you designate. I will get several if necessary.

I am so pleased to finally be able to bring this to completion. I know it must have been frustrating to you to have this take so long and to have us seen to be so unresponsive. I hope this totally enthusiastic ending makes up for all of that!

Your friend in Alpena:

- Carol Shafto

## After The Fall

On the day of ratification or passing of the resolution for sister city relationship between Alpena and the two above villages several speakers were heard. These included, among many, Penny Boldrey, Mr. Tom Ray, two student representatives who visited Gambia in May 2005 and Dr. Avery Aten.

This was buffered by loop of fifty photos of the villages taken by the student while in the Gambia. At the end of the presentation Mayor John F. gimlet read into the record the above proclamation and vote was tabled to pass it.

This Sister City proclamation between Alpena with Njawara/Kinte Kunda, Lower Badibou District, the Gambia was moved by Councilwoman Carol Shaftu, seconded by Councilman Karschnick, that the proclamation to establish a sister city program with the villages of Njwara and Kinte Kunda be approved. The move was carried by unanimous vote.

A copy of the sister City Resolution passed by Alpena City Council on December $5^{th}$ 2005 is reproduced for your pleasure to read.

Dr. Alhasan Sisawo Ceesay, MD

Chapter 11

PROCLAMATION TO ESTABLISH A "SISTER CITY" PROGRAM WITH NJAWARA AND KINTE KUNDA, LWER BADIBOU DISTRICT, GAMBIA, WEST AFRICA

WHEREAS, the City of Alpena recognises and supports the concept of global cooperation and community; and

WHERAS, the villagers of Njawara and Kinte Kunda, through their local leaders and Dr. Alhasan S. Ceesay, have reached out their hand in friendship and goodwill, and

WHEREAS, relationships were established by students and faculty of Alpena Community College when they were warmly welcomed to the villages for a service project earlier this year, and

WHEREAS, mutual understanding of our diversities as well as our similarities and the cultural exchanges that will result, will be beneficial to the citizens of both areas, and

WHEREAS, true global community is often established one person at a time, and one city and village at a time, leading to beneficial relations and programs for all;

## After The Fall

NOW, THEREFORE, I, John F. Gilmet, by virtue of the authority vested in me as Mayor, DO HEREBY PROCLAIM, a "Sister City" Program with the villages of

NJAWARA/KINTE KUNDA

LOWER BADIBOU DISTRICT

GAMBIA

And urge all area citizens to extend the hand of fellowship and an embrace of genuine fraternity to their friends in NJAWARA/KINTE KINTE KUNDA and pledge support and loyalty as these communities of two great nations join together as "Sister Cities"

Signed at Alpena Michigan, United States of America, on this $5^{th}$ day of December, 2005. Councilwoman Carol Shafto read the following reply from me to Council and residents of Alpena City.

## Dr. Alhasan Sisawo Ceesay, MD

ALPENA, THANKS FOR TWINING WITH US

Honourable Mayor John F. Gilmet, Alpena City Council and residents of Alpena; please allow me convey heartfelt thanks as well as greetings from the Commissioner, NBD, Kerewan Area Council, the Chief of Lower Badibou, the Alkalos (village heads) of Njawara and Kinte Kunda.

I am today full of joy and gratitude for twining resolution ratified by the Alpena City Council. I am speechless as one of my dreams for the villager and America has now materialized in this twining resolution passed by Alpena. We are two good people now merged in good will for humanity and friendship. This coming together will archive a lot for both of us.

There is a lot for us to gain as well as learn from each other and generations to come will thank us for having taken the first footsteps of bringing people of diverse cultures and understanding together.

Enclosed is message from the Gambia in response to the most welcomed news in your last email. This is the top of the iceberg for there is lot more benefit in this act. In addition, as long as I am alive Alpena and Gambia will not only benefit from this unique venture but will smile yearly for having dreamt along with me.

## After The Fall

Let me, in passing, mention with thanks the first harbingers of this day. They are Mr. Thomas P. Ray and his Leadership team of students from Alpena Community College who visited Njawara village in May 2005.

Thomas Ray and the students laid the marvellous foundation we today concretize. Mrs. Penny Boldrey and Mathew Dunckel deserve our appreciation for remaining interested and in constant contact with me.

The Gambia, the district authority of Lower Badibou and villagers remain eternally grateful for giving us the chance of twining with you. A Huge thanks Alpena City, the Mayor of Alpena and Alpena City Council for work well done. Councilwoman Mrs.

Carol Shafto who relentlessly steered the twining proposal to completion also deserves our profound gratitude. The villagers and I are eternally indebted to all at Alpena. In addition, we look forward to working hand in hand for the reward of all parties.

Finally, I would again like to pay tribute to past and present friends at Alpena who helped me reach this pedestal. All of you helped make my sojourn to America a remarkable success. I would like many more of my friends to be like you at Alpena.

Dr. Alhasan Sisawo Ceesay, MD

I hope you will believe, as well as join me, in my dream of providing modern medical aid to the Gambian villagers. Thanks a million and God bless America!

Signed: DR. ALHASAN SISAWO CEESAY, MD

FOUNDER/COORDINATOR

MANDING MEDICAL CENTRE

NJAWARA, THE GAMBIA

Two weeks later I received three copies of the "sister City Proclamation" along with a video tape of the Alpena City Council Meeting of December 5, 2005. Also enclosed were the Alpena news and copy of Alpena Public Notices showing minutes of the City Council meeting which carried ratification of the sister city proclamation by a unanimous vote.

I must confess exhilaration in my heart for Alpena City Council having done so much for my villages without reservation and accomplished with great speed. I sent the following communiqué to the current representative to the Gambia, Ambassador Joseph D. Stafford in preparing them for the arrival the package from the Alpena City Council for forwarding to the Commissioner of the North Bank Division, the Gambia.

After The Fall

MANDING MEDICAL CENTRE

245 Great Western Street

Manchester M14 4LQ
Email: alhasanceesay@hotmail.com

Date: 10/12/05

Ambassador Joseph D. Stafford

Embassy of the United States of America

Kairaba Avenue

P. M. Box 19

Banjul, the Gambia,

West Africa

RE: Manding Medical Centre/Alpena USA Twining

Dear Ambassador Stafford,

I am Dr. Alhasan S. Ceesay from Njawara village and currently on studies in the UK. This is to introduce the above self-help health organisation at Njawara as well as kindly request favour of your good office's service in behalf Alpena Michigan and the villages of Njawara and Kinte Kunda, the Gambia.

## Dr. Alhasan Sisawo Ceesay, MD

I pioneered the above centre, after graduating as a doctor and upon returning to the Gambia in 1992. It became an NGO in 1994 after being fully registered by the Justice Department and recognised by the Ministry of Health in 1993.

In addition, we are now a registered Charitable Trust, as Friends of Manding, in England and Wales by the Charity Commission of the UK. Our website is: www.friendsofmandinggambimed.btck.co.uk . or www.publishkunsa.com . It will show our home page as "Friends of Manding." Alternatively, one can used a short cut by typing in "Manding Medical Centre, Njawara" and click search. The same home page plus lot more will appear.

I have also written two books and a hefty portion of proceed from the sale of both books is earmarked to help support Manding Medical Centre at Njawara and our goal of providing medical aid to the villager, especially children.

More information about my work and commitment to providing much needed medical service to the region in conjunction with the Gambia Ministry of Health can be seen in our website as above.

## AFTER THE FALL

Finally, I am more than delighted to report that Alpena City, Michigan, USA has just ratified a sister city program with my home village Njawara and Kinte Kunda village in the Lower Badibou District, North Bank Division, the Gambia.

Hence, I have asked the Alpena City Mayor's Office to send five copies of the final proclamation declaring the sister city status between Alpena and the above two named villages in Badibou to you for your office to kindly deliver the documents to the Commissioner North Bank Division at Kerewan.

Thank you for taking time to assist us in the above matter. Please feel free to contact me any time convenient to you. Best wishes for good health and achievement in the coming year. Regard to your family.

Yours Sincerely

Dr. Alhasan S. Ceesay, MD

Founder/Coordinator

Manding Medical Centre

Njawara, The Gambia, West Africa.

This letter was followed with two telephone calls to the Embassy of the United States in the Gambia to verify receipt of the package sent from Alpena to Joseph D.

## DR. ALHASAN SISAWO CEESAY, MD

Stafford. The Secretary to Mr. Stafford, in the last phone call let me know it usually take a month or more before none official mail arrives at their desk.

He assured me that the office will do as request whenever the package reaches the Embassy. I called Sefo Fafanding Kinte and Alkalo Hadi Panneh and told them to check with either Ambassador Joseph Stafford directly or one of the officers in the know at the office for their copies of the sister city proclamation of which the villagers are unsung heroes for having received the ACC students who visited Njawara in May 2005 with open hearts, hospitality, generosity and warmth.

It was not until Thursday, February 16$^{th}$, 2006 that Ambassador Joseph D. Stafford and team where able to deliver, in person amid tumultuous reception and celebration, the sister-city proclamation between Alpena City, Michigan USA, with Njawara and Kinte Kunda villages in the North Bank of the Gambia.

I made it clear that the brief ceremony at Njawara on the 16/2/06 marked the end of phase one of the sister city relationship between us and Alpena Michigan. I suggested the following four areas for food for thought by all concern. They are:-

After The Fall

1. Education

This already started in earnest as some in Alpena have expressed desire to sponsor worthy candidates at the primary level for an experimental period of one year. Higher levels, such as college education and nursing training and or other relevant skill areas will in due course be included.

2. Health

A lot is planned for health oriented programs and Manding Medical Centre will be enhanced to a much functional status. There will be training programs for health personnel etc.

3. Tourism: I am studying ways of creating tourist attraction with facilities erected in due course to the region.

4. Cultural: Exchanges entailing having cultural dance troop(s) from the Lower Badibou District travel to Alpena Michigan, and other cities in the USA during the summers to display our fabric of entertainment, history and arts.

Dr. Alhasan Sisawo Ceesay, MD

These are few ideas in the pipeline. Feel free to add yours to enrich the program. This is by no means binding or final but seeking more suggestions on how to benefit both parties in this unique twining program just approved by Alpena City. Let me make it crystal clear that there is no financial commitment from Alpena.

However, the cultural show can raise lot of money upon performing in America. I thanked the Commissioner North Bank, Sefo of Lower Badibou, District Authority and Kerewan Area Council for having worked so hard with me to provide this excellent opportunity to our people. I promised that more is on the way.

Three weeks earlier I received this e-mail from Councilwoman Mrs. Carol Shafto announcing the good news of her efforts. "Dr. Ceesay, we have sent five copies of the proclamation to the America Embassy- which you provided the address for.

I also have three copies of the proclamation for you as well as a copy of the tape of the meeting; a copy of the newspaper where the action appeared; and a copy of the newspaper with the official minutes. I will get these out to you today.

## After The Fall

It was a most wonderful evening as you will see on the tape. Five people, your friends old and new, spoke in favour of the proclamation. This included Dr. Avery Aten who I have now spoken with and who is very enthusiastic about working on the medical aspect of things with you.

He will be in touch with you by phone he said. But you will be able to see him and hear what he had to say during City Council meeting of December 5, 2005. Also speaking where two students who have visited the Gambia; Tom Ray and Penny Boldrey. (And me, of course).

I read your wonderful letter for the record. We also had a loop of over fifty slides showing on the screen during the presentation. It was the nicest sister-city ceremony we have ever had-by far! Usually we just read the proclamation and that is it.

I think this ends my part in all of this-except for one thing. My sons and I were going to "adopt" a family through Save the Children. This involves sending a letter each month and with an amount of money.

We would be happy to adopt some children from your village instead if there is an easy way to do this. We would need a name and address and what form we could make our donation in (money order?).

Dr. Alhasan Sisawo Ceesay, MD

We are not really wealthy- but could send $20 -$25 a month for at least a year to a deserving child. Of course; we would hope that they might send a note now and then... but this all up to you.

I hope you are pleased with all that has happened.

I remained your friend.

Carol Shafto.

In reply I sent my friend Carol Shafto the following.

Hello Carol; Now I am able to response to your email. First, please accept our eternal ineptness' for having worked so hard to bring the twining into reality. Only God can reward your efforts. Please kindly extend our heartfelt gratitude to the Mayor and your fellow Councillors at Alpena.

Send me the Mayor's telephone. I need to convey our appreciation to him. I had a long chat with the village and they were in cloud nine about the approval of the sister city program.

I will be forwarding the names of deserving school children you might want to sponsor/adopt. I will cal you, before forwarding the names, about it when I get the list that the parents and headmaster promised to send me.

After The Fall

Thanks a million and God blesses you and yours. Best wishes for good health and successful 2006. I look forward to our travelling to the Gambia soon. Regard.

Sincerely

Dr. Alhasan S. Ceesay, MD

In the mean time Mrs. Penny Boldrey was also busy doing a story for the ACC Alumni News. In addition Carol was able to have a feature about the just approved sister city program done by the local news paper. She was very happy about it as the email bellow from Carol shows.

"Good Morning Alhasan, "our story" is headline, above the fold, in the Alpena News today! It is wonderful publication for your project.

I will send you copies but you can read it on-line today only at www.thealpenanews.com. It reads "Alpena's sister-city- ACC graduate initiates partnership with Gambia villages." And there is a wonderful colour picture of one of the ACC students with village children.

I hope you enjoyed the story and are pleased with my efforts for publicity. The news reporter, Sue Lutuszek, will do a follow-up story about people "adopting Children for education purposes", like I am doing with my son(s).

Dr. Alhasan Sisawo Ceesay, MD

It is a good day for celebration. Check the website.

Your friend

Carol

Here is one of several features about the twining between Alpena City with Njwara and Kinte Kunda villages in the North Bank Division, the Gambia.

ALPENA NEWS MICHIGAN, USA

SISTER CITY PROGRAM HAS TIES TO

ACC STUDENT OF 1960s

A link dating back to the 1960s has helped Alpena establish a sister city program with Njawara and Kinte Kunda, Lower Badibou District, the Gambia.

The program was initiated by Alhasan Ceesay, MD, an Alpena Community College of the 1960s and the 2005 Distinguished Graduate who lives in the Wes African country. He was assisted by ACC staff and Councilwoman Carol Shafto.

"He feels this is his American home and villages in Gambia are his African home and wanted to link the two together." Carol Shafto said.

## After The Fall

When Penny Boldrey of the ACC Foundation first put Ceesay in touch with Shafto for assistance in the venture, Shafto was leery of his intentions.

"I did not get it," she said. "I wanted to know what we are going to gain?" the whole idea is simply to put out information on the situation in those villages in the public eye, Shafto said Ceesay's dream is to build a medical centre to serve the villages, since care is many miles away and roads in and out of villages aren't passable by ambulance.

Currently patients are transported out of villages without ambulances for distances to health centres from their homes. Avery Aten, MD, of Alpena also has become involved with the project.

"The medical aspects of this relationship can be long-term," he told city council members. He said so medical statistics regarding the area, such as the average life expectancy is 53 years old and 85 out of 1000 children die during birth.

According to Shafto, some of Aten's hopes include sending medical equipment which is no longer used here to the villages and even possibly having nursing students experiencing practicing there.

## Dr. Alhasan Sisawo Ceesay, MD

"I just see all kinds of goodwill things happening," Shafto said. "For us to have the opportunity to lead about a totally different culture is good for us."

"One aspect Shafto highlighted is the opportunity for elementary classroom in Alpena to communicate with the village school.

Although she assisted in having the proclamation made, Shafto gives credit for making it happen to individuals at ACC.

"My part is minor compared to what ACC has done," she said. "They are the ones who really got this started."

During the trip the students met with various village leaders who showed them what projects they were working on and where the greatest need was. In addition, the students taught some short classes on the United States.

One day the group helped with the construction of a mosque. They also visited the agricultural centre and health centre.

Ray said the trip "contributed greatly" in making the sister city proclamation a reality "because it gave people in Alpena a connection to the village."

After The Fall

"The Gambia District Authority of Lower Badibou and villagers remain eternally grateful for giving us chance of twining with you.

Huge thanks to the City of Alpena, Mayor of Alpena and Alpena City Council," Alhasan wrote. "The villagers and I are eternally indebted to all at Alpena. In addition, we look forward to working hand in hand for reward of all parties."

-Sue Latuszek: The Alpena News 2005-

The first hatchling of this merging of diverse hearts is as follows:-

Njawara Basic School

Lower Badibou District

North Bank Division

The Gambia, W. Africa

19/01/06


Dear Sir/Madam

RE: To whom it may concern.

Dr. Alhasan Sisawo Ceesay, MD

These students are promising students whose parents are not able to fully support their educational needs. As a result, we would be very grateful if a concern person(s) can assist the students and their parents in taking care of some of the financial difficulties they are encountering to earn education.

These include school fees, uniforms, book bills and other school needs. Thank you and in anticipation, I remain,

Yours Faithfully

Lamin K. Juwara

Principal

These where the initial list of needy student to benefit from what was going to be the Manding Medical Centre/USA scholarship grants.

| NAME ADDRESS | AGE | CLASS | PARENT |
|---|---|---|---|
| 1. Ismaila Ceesay Njawara | 14yrs | 8B | Dodu Ceesay |
| 2. Edrisa Barry Njawara | 14yrs | 8B | Adoulie Barry |
| 3. Alieu Dem Njawara | 12yrs | 7B | Modou Dem |

## After The Fall

4. Mamud Panneh    12yrs    7A    Ousainu Panneh    jawara

5. Adama Jallow    12yrs    7B    Assan Jallow    Ker Ardo

6. Kally Bah    13yrs    8B    Saikou Bah    Ker Ardo

7. Njammeh Bah    12yrs    7B    Musa Bah    Toro Bah

8. Hammed Dem    12yrs    7B    Musa I. Bah    Toro Bah

9. Ebrima Kanteh    15yrs    7B    Baboucar Kaneh    Toro Bah

10. Mustapha Jawo    15yrs    8A    Omar Jawo    Toro Bah

11. Modou Touray    11yrs    6A    Sohna Jaw    Panneh Bah

12. Nuha Krubally    10yrs    5A    Modo Krubally    Samba Musu

13. Matarr Panneh    10yrs    4B    Bora Panneh    Njawara

14. Modou Loum    14yrs    7B    Bintou Jammeh    Ker Jebal

Dr. Alhasan Sisawo Ceesay, MD

The above list and letter were faxed to Councilwoman Carol Shafto on the 23/02/06. The fax simply read:-

Hi Carol, I hope you are okay and back at work. I hereby forward a list of school children from Njawara school needing sponsorship. Feel free to contact those you think would like to participate in this educational project. The first three candidates in the list are earmarked for you and your son(s). See names 1 – 3 in the list.

Send all monies via Western Union in the name of Aja Hadi Panneh, (Alkalo of Njawara village) to any Gambian Bank that Western Union deals with in Gambia. Then email me stating amounts, date sent and for who. I will follow up by contacting the Principal of Njawara School, the parents and the chief of the district to ascertain prompt and proper distribution.

In addition, I will have Aja Hadi Panneh (Alkalo), the parents, Headmaster and were possible the recipient students to write acknowledging the amounts received. Please feel free to contact me if you have any questions or ideas to promote the above noble educational commitment. Once again, thanks and we remain grateful for your stand.

Your Friend

Dr. Alhasan S. Ceesay, MD

# After The Fall

## Chapter 12

### PROFILES OF HEROINES WHO CHAMPIONED MY SUCCESS

I pray that my readers would kindly allow me indulge in a moment of sentimentality in writing about the following magnanimous ladies who not only shaped my life but sacrificed all they had to let me succeed in this life.

First and foremost of all is my mother, Mrs. Famatanding Tarawaleh, without whose love and devotion my twin brother and I would never been on this planet nor about all that you now know about me to have come to light.

To us Africans every day is mothers and fathers day for one cannot repay the love, guiding and education parents gave while we were but fledglings. Mother epitomizes, love, caring, kindness and ability to share with others. She believed in teamwork co-operated with all the wives in the compound.

Her warmth and charm made it comfortable for others to relate to her as well as confined in her. I have already said a lot about mother in my first book, "The legend against all odds". So I will not bore those who already have a copy of the afore mentioned book.

Dr. Alhasan Sisawo Ceedsay, MD

However I would like to reiterate that mother was an excellent one we would not exchange at any time for any reason and she had fulfil beyond doubts all that was expected of a mother.

She contributed immensely to my primary school education and helped me ply through battle I waged against my father' perception with regards to schooling and Western morals. She was instrumental in making it possible for me to have the right to Western education.

I am grateful that the world welcomed me through loving heart and endearment of my mother. I am certain she is not the least disappointed on my stance in this life's sojourn. I am my mother as much as my father is.

They were good springboards from which to take off in today's world. She sadly departed this life at the age of 89 years of glorious village life. Mother's passing left us very lonely and missing her dearly.

The second lady of note and indeed one that had influenced my medical aspiration was none other than Grandma Sallah Hanti Sey. She was a renowned herbalist of her time from the Fulani region of Bundu in Senegal.

## After The Fall

I was her protégée and lieutenant at work at the tender age of six. We would go deep into the bush harvesting herbs, roots, leafs and backs of trees from various plants to be used for medicinal purpose.

I now wished that I was, at that tender age, able to compile the names of the plants she used to treat yellow fever, measles, diarrhoea, malaria and dengue fever. Boy! Her portions would stop most diseases as soon as the patient took them.

I barely recall the concoctions but their results remain vivid and clear in my memory of those years. I had no idea of the importance of what she was engaged but the crystal ball becomes clearer and obvious when one recalls the sheer numbers of people from far and wide who would walk hundreds of miles to seek treatment from her.

The amazing thing about this unique lady was that she was so accommodating and never charged a penny or cent for service rendered to her patients. Some would insist that she accept the goat or sheep they brought along with them. Her final act to such requests would be to kill the beast and let the patients feed on it while undergoing treatment.

Dr. Alhasan Sisawo Ceesay, MD

Her home was always packed with patients arriving at different times of the day. She would today be nick named mother Theresa because of her ability to cope with these influxes.

Grand ma was a reference book' a bundle of joy and love to young ones like me. She sang lullabies to soothe children. And told endless spell bounding stories about African Kings, their wealth and the way they extended their realms that left the listener envious.

These stories kept many listening children at times petrified, scared or cry out of sympathy for the fate of the characters in her stories. She even told of stories about Africans carrying loads of gold on horse, mules and slaves across the Sahara to Egypt and also of how they help the great king of that land build colossal building pointing to the sky. We now assume these to be the wonderful pyramid adorning Egypt.

Her embrace was a welcomed relief and sought panacea that sends the toddler to sleep. It was just too cuddling and comfortable and we used to run to be with her as soon as she appears. People, lately, used to tease me that grand ma Sallah's kindness might have rubbed on me.

## After The Fall

They just would not understand that I am no clone of her but want to good and share my life and skill with others. They see my local village health organization being not only an off shoot of her herbalist days but also a fulfilment of her wish for the region.

She had three sons and a girl. None of who took interest in her herbalist career. She died peacefully in her sleep at the age of 92 years of fruitful life indeed. Her daughter, Mrs. Fatou Sallah Ceesay, was the youngest of grandma's children and lived in Banjul, the capital city of the Gambia.

It was at this untiring lady's place that I stayed after my high school days and part of the time when I was doing my nursing training at the Royal Victoria Hospital, Banjul. She was kind and protective of me out fear that city life would ruin me.

Seven of us crowded her room and the okay kraal was much fun to be at. This lady would get up at 5 AM and prepare our breakfast, pull out the uniforms of those still going to school for me to ready the children for school. Fatou Sallah Ceesay would be at the school gate selling food or fruits to the children for breakfast.

Dr. Alhasan Sisawo Ceesay, MD

And during break hour she would sell pancake and locally made soft drinks etc to those who could not have breakfast at home because of distance and transportation problem to and from the school grounds. Her earning tops of the money needed to feed the troops in her house. She too had influenced me greatly and I miss her greatly. She died three years before my 1979 visit to Gambia.

The other female member of the family that had profound effect on my life is my elder sister Binta Ceesay. She was credited for spectacularly rescuing me from the dead when I was left in a basket outside of the house to be buried as stillbirth the next day.

As folklore has it I was born lifeless and only made feeble cries after 5 Am which led my sister to pick me from the basket and return me to mother to be breast fed. By so doing this lady saved my life and I remain eternally grateful to her. She cared and helped me bond with the other siblings after the death of my twin brother. We got even closer as grown-ups did.

I still confide in her and Binta Ceesay remains an integral part of the day to day life of Njawara Ceesay Kunda. She has always been supportive of my goals and advises when needed.

## After The Fall

When it comes to having things done then the scale tips toward Binta Ceesay. The principle of love and respect towards others make her relationship with the family, friends, and villagers admirable.

As a result of which she became the magnet towards which everyone is pulled. Proverbs 16:32 in the bible says, "He that is slow to anger is better than a mighty man, and he that is controlling his spirit than the one capturing a city." It is fair to freely say that Binta Ceesay belong to this mould. Her cool and calm nature brings her many friends anywhere she goes.

Binta once told me that having an insight and understanding of a situation makes you see the likely reason (s) for confrontation and one can prevent anger from flaring and distorting the main cause of a row. She always warns me against becoming lazy.

She paraphrased it by saying that "God works in mysterious ways but one must be willing to help God's hand and desire for you." She stressed that I must work hard to earn my own living and that I should never give deaf ears to criticism. It helps us see what others could not and thereby turns us into better and wise achievers. Finally she advised that I remain steadfast with my faith at all times.

Dr. Alhasan Sisawo Ceesay, MD

The pillar of my success goes to none other than my wife Mrs. Fatou Koma-Ceesay who changed the course of life for the better. She is the jewel and coronet of the crown of a host of heroines that reach the summit of the highest peak of mountain life.

She is the unique person that gave me romantic love without asking for guarantees of benefit in return for her commitment to being my wife. Fatou is radiant at heart and deed. Fatou is my soul and she is mine even in death. Ours was love from first sight that never faded but grew daily for both of us to the present.

Romantic fantasies of life reconcile in this lady. She stands out in my heart and emotion and is the beauty of the world in my eyes. Fatou is stunningly beautiful, young, sexy, intelligent and all I wanted in a woman. She is much more than a feeling, which removes protective barriers one may have erected.

She was unquestionable the love I yearned for and she made me finally realise a soothing or comfort and sharing I hardly experienced since reaching manhood. As time went on we developed and matured into twins that loved, share everything and struggled in life. This beauty lived through thick and thin of my seesawing life.

## After The Fall

One look at Fatou will allow you class her as the queen of the palace of queens. With her beauty goes an exceptionally well-mannered sociable and intelligent lady. We now have three beautiful daughters, Famatanding Ceesay, Binta Ceesay and Roheyata Ceesay, who are as brilliant as their mother.

I am yet to hear anyone making objectionable remarks about my dream girl. Having Fatou Koma-Ceesay as my wife and mother of my children makes me feel very happy likewise born lucky. I am just hoping to be able to compensate her impact on my life by being a worthy husband to her at all times.

The rest of my heroines are from lands beyond the Dark Continent. They each were left at awc upon learning about my struggles and the path my desire to have Western education led. So I present to you my American and British heroines starting at Alpena Community College (ACC) in 1967.

I arrive at this college having lost my sponsor and the college was about to send me back to the Gambia for lack of financial support. It was then that Mrs. Viola S. Glennie, then a professor of foreign language, came to my rescue without my knowledge of her benevolence.

Dr. Alhasan Sisawo Ceesay, MD

She was also my teacher for I had enrolled in her French class. She and her husband, late Judge Philip Glennie, were the first to response to appeals to make it possible for me to continue at the college. She was very instrumental in having Alpena ladies Association donate £400 towards my studies at Alpena Community College.

We became even greater friends as time went on. She and her husband would take me out on weekends and tried everything they could to soften the blow of disappointment I ran into as a first entrant to America.

She was very sorry and flabbergasted on hearing the unbelievable effort I put in other to have the right to Western Education. My relationship with the Glennies grew and she remained in touch with me at all my world travels. She has now returned in peace to her maker happy that I kept my covenant with my people in Africa.

I left them to complete my studies at Olivet College and at Michigan Technological University in Houghton, Michigan. The Glennies were my American "mum and dad" and I miss them very much." God rests their souls in heaven. Amen! The first American family at whose home I stayed the first two weeks in Alpena was at the Riggs.

## After The Fall

They lived at 240 Washington Avenue in Alpena in Michigan. Mrs. Rita Riggs and husband owned an Ice-cream pallor down town Alpena. I was the second of two Africans that ever lodged at their home while attending ACC. The First was Mr. Eric Gabba from Ghana and did engineering courses at the college.

Even though my bus arrived very late, around 1:45 AM, Ritha Riggs was there waiting to welcome me at her plush home. I was ushered into their mansion and offered a glass of fresh milk to quench my thirst.

At the same time a table was set for me to have some food before retiring to bed. I stayed with the Riggs from 19 August to the 9$^{th}$ of September 1967 when I had to move to Russell Wilson Hall as then required of all foreign students attending ACC.

Mean while Mrs. Rita became "MUM" for short. She was a wingless angel in a human body. Always smiling and ready to offer assistance any time one needs it. She treated me as one of her own from day one of my meeting the family in 1967. And she and her family were marvelours friends to me.

Dr. Alhasan Sisawo Ceesay, MD

She and her husband Howard Riggs helped a lot with part of my tuition for that term at Alpena Community College. I felt sad that I had to be at the dormitory my first year at the college. The Riggs moved out of Alpena six months after I met them.

We kept in touch until my return to the Gambia when I lost contact as all letters to them were returned by the U. S. post office. I learnt from a friend that one of their younger daughters is now a nurse at Alpena General. I shall follow this lead to re-link with my past and first American family. Mrs. Rita and Her husband Howard Riggs I learnt are no longer with us.

Next is Mrs. Magritte Cruise, a resident of Alpena, Michigan and one of the schoolteachers. I met her when my financial state had plummeted to zero level with all my former supporters having left the college. Upon hearing about my circumstances she volunteered to lodge me for rest of my studies at the college.

Her husband works as an engineer with the Jesse Beset foundation in Alpena. Magritte love debates and so we used to discuss about Africa, politics, education, conservation, family planning and the pill, among other topics into the wee hours of the night.

## After The Fall

Her children also used to bombard me with all sorts of question about the African way of life and especially those of their age group. Sometimes these kids sound more like the entire continent comprised of only the Tarzan images they picked up from misinformation by the telecast entertainment on adventure into the jungles of Africa.

At times, I just let them know that Africa was a vast land far bigger than the USA with thousands of cultures and tribes. No one knows all about everyone they may come across in books. This made them believe that I might just come from Detroit, Michigan for according to them I do not dress like the typical pictures of Africans they see in moves or on television.

And to make matters worse I spoke English well and understood it without the "afro-American" accent. So Magritte and I had to do much better job in convincing those youngsters that I was indeed the real thing from the Mandinka tribe in Gambia.

Let me come back to Mrs. Magritte Cruise who in her own right was a generous and very forthright person. She too organised groups for me to talk to about the Gambia and how I got into primary school and eventually landing into Alpena Michigan.

Dr. Alhasan Sisawo Ceesay, MD

She said, "We could not ever dream of having someone so far away to choose to start college at so remote a place like Alpena. You must be very daring after all the stories about the KKK and blacks etc.

Did this ever cross your mind?" I replied that a mountain climber never fears falling because the possibility is there; besides if we do not go out and seek for our people who will do it for us. Did Christopher Combo felt scared using the Nina Santa Maria and the Pinta to set sail in search trade in East India?

I can tell you I had a unique experience with Cruises and was very happy to dispel a lot assumed believe about African and Africa. Magritte and her husband Bill Cruise were very much the push that led to my having a partial scholarship from the Jesse Besse foundation to help me continue drive to take the golden flees back to the Gambia.

Another unique heroine who helped me while the going was very unbearable was a nurse, Mrs. Geraldine Shepherd; I met while working as an assistant nurse on a summer job at St. Joseph Hospital, Flint Michigan in 1970. She became involve out of sheer sympathy upon learning about the sorry state my life succumbed in the summer of 1970.

## After The Fall

It was then that she learnt from friends that I spent nights at rat infested basement someone rented to me for ten dollars a week and that rats have been nibbling my feet while I am asleep. There was great fear that I might get infected from such encounters.

There was no shower facility so I used to sneak into the hospital and have quick wash before someone notice. My meagre weekly pay was not going to support luxury and I needed a bundle to pay for the $6000 tuition fees and this excluded the cost for the dormitory, books, meals, and transportation fees.

She got me out of my misery after discussing my state with her husband Mr. Homer Shepherd. They agreed to offer me one of their empty rooms free of charge for the rest of that summer. I remain thankful for their kindness and understanding which helped me raise money for my schooling that year.

The summer; although started with hard and difficult moments, ended joyfully with the Shepherds. This benevolent family even asked nurses to contribute to a secrete package present they were preparing for me to take along at the end of the summer.

## Dr. Alhasan Sisawo Ceesay, MD

We have since been constantly in touch and their home became my home anytime that I pass through Flint. Again, I remain profoundly grateful to the Shepherds for being so kind and helpful to my mission in 1970. They helped me cross the challenge I faced in Flint, Michigan in 1970.

I fell into trouble on returning to Africa to start medical schooling in Liberia. Political disturbance in both Gambia and Liberia led to my return to the USA December 1981. Lot about this has been documented in my first book so to cut a long story short; the INS in Detroit refused my request and gave me fifteen days in which to leave the U.S.A.

Faced with this pending denial of my request back in 1982, I walked into the hallowed halls of St. Paul's Cathedral diocese of Michigan in Detroit searching for sanctuary and help with litigation against the INS. I actually miss took that cathedral as being a Catholic mission in Detroit.

My reasons for coming to Detroit were very clear. It was the days of doubts about not only my future but also those of Africa. It was in those sorrowful hay days when politicians and military men and their juntas wreck innocent lives thoughtlessly.

## After The Fall

American sense of justice was the only humane salvation, if not the only avenue of hope left to me. After a few hurried flights, on April 15$^{th}$ 1982, I was on the second floor where Hugh Davis introduced me Mrs. Patricia Koblyski, Pat for short, the then refugee co-ordinator for the Diocese of Michigan in Detroit, Michigan.

Over a grim blackness of an impending denial of my request Mrs. Koblyski as you will soon find out was god sent angel to soften my fall. Once in her office, Pat stopped her typing and asked what help she could offer me. I narrated my experience and mission in such nervous way that she had literally held me to reassure me that she cares.

I showed her the INS letter notifying me it intention to deny my request for asylum in America. I gave her all news clippings we had about the coup in the Gambia and the Government's reaction upon reinstated back to power by the Senegalese Forces. Pat read everything given her and then called Rev. Hughes White, advisor to the Bishop, who came to join us right away.

Pat, Hughes and Virgil Jones and I went over all details of my plight and the eminent dangers ahead if forced to return to the Gambia prematurely. At times I broke into tears and later pick up my sanity and continue telling my sad experience and loss I encountered since 1981.

Dr. Alhasan Sisawo Ceesay, MD

That very day Pat, with the blessings of Bishop Coleman McGehee, set up would become the Ceesay Committee to help me fight my pending denial case at the Detroit Immigration and Naturalisation Service (INS). This committee became the brains behind my fight with the INS courts.

Without Pat's initial involvement life would have turned for the worse. She relentlessly fought for my freedom until her untimely death, which left me sad, shocked and bewildered. Patricia Koblski was a good friend who cried with me and at the same time wiped my tears.

She gave me hope of freedom and assisted entire villages and me several thousand miles away. She knew none of these people but like the rest of Diocese of Michigan was more than dedicated in seeing that we all breathe the air in peace and walk together side by side in freedom on mother earth. Patricia Koblynski, thanks a million for living a full Christian life and for all of us. Our profound gratitude and indebtedness goes to you for being our Good Samaritan.

The only benefiting legacy I have for you and my villagers is returning to serve the Gambia and especially the villagers for whom you fought so hard during these last minutes of a true Christian and wonderful life of giving to others.

## After The Fall

My villagers and I will never forget you or kindness you bestowed us. Let us now reflect a bit on Mrs. Lois R. Leonard, Editor of the Diocesan Newspaper the Record. Lot was said about this wingless American Angel in my first book.

Let me reiterate that Lois is a human rights advocate and a dedicated journalist interested in the struggles of the under developed world and the downtrodden. She was one that would stand between a giant and midget to protect the latter, if she felt the midget being right, weakling from being crushed.

Lois Leonard does not hesitate to call a spayed a spayed or attention to miss use of authority or responsibility wherever it occurs. Despite this stance, Lois was a kind-hearted lady more than willing to share with others. She champions freedom of expression and human rights for all of us.

She came on board the Ceesay Committee as soon as she heard of my troubles and never missed a single meeting of the committee's four years of life. Mrs. Lois Leonard was an asset that kept our meetings lively and balanced.

She never hesitated for one moment in putting her point across or that in suggesting new approaches she feels convince would push our goal forward. In short, Lois was one of our respected think tanks in those days and it was through her that we were able to engage the services of Professor Francis Conti of Detroit College of Law.

She wrote lots of articles about my plight spear heading appeals for support and asked for help both to the committee's drive and me to bring relief to my predicaments. She remained loyal to the cause until her death in 1989 when I had moved to Montserrat in the West Indies. Before then she kept the lines of communication between us open and would once on a while send me money to help with the little mundane needs as she called them.

Meet Mrs. Lorna V. Robinson, Britain's crown-less queen. I met this angel through her nursing job in 1991 at the Colchester General Hospital while I was a trainee doctor doing my clinical clerkship at the hospital. We have been friends since then and for those who read my first book will understand the uniqueness of the giving lady.

## After The Fall

Lorna and her husband Keith are regular visitors to the Gambia and have been to my place in Gambia on several occasions. Lorna helped christen my first child, Famatanding Ceesay, while we were in Colchester, Essex County in 1991. She also was the first to show interest in the self-help village health organisation (Manding Medical Centre) I set up at Njawara village in the Gambia.

She and her husband were key to the formation of the Friends of Manding, which is an off shoot of Manding Medical Centre at Njawara. Doctors, nurses, and residents of Colchester who frequently visit the Gambia form the Friends of Manding.

Two of the most prominent trustee of Friends of Manding have been to Njawara village and returned convinced that the centres stand was for a worthy cause and service to the villagers. Lorna frequently sent me small packages of medicines and equipment to help our service at Njawara.

Mrs. Lorna Robinson serves as the secretary and Keith as Chairman of Friends of Manding. Lorna never stopped from being in touch with us when we returned to the Gambia. She was very kind to invite my wife and I to attend weeding ceremonies of her younger daughter, Miss Fiona Robinson to Mr. Reeves Watson.

## Dr. Alhasan Sisawo Ceesay, MD

I stayed at the Robinsons after the wedding and started the trail you just read about in previous chapters. I left for London when the health of the Robinsons was not able to endure. I was just comfortable watching break their backs day after day to keep me sheltered and fed. So I had to leave Colchester voluntarily for London February 2002.

Lorna a unique, kind-hearted, hard working tireless heroine one never forgets. She is an early bird that burns the midnight oil daily in an effort to seek help for the Manding Medical Centre and the villagers at Njawara in the Gambia. As a nurse she carries her duties with diligence and tact that only Angels like her can deliver.

Lorna is charming, likeable, cheerful, free spirit and a friend one yearns to have. Most are home with her within few minutes of coming to know her. She is well versed politically about event in the developing and developed world and a socially amiable lady. Lorna goes beyond all expectation to reach out and help the needy, especially Gambian villagers.

She is my ray of hope in the dark bowels of a foreign land. Pope John Paul (Albino Lucciano) said "A wise man does not allow him-self to be dogged by appearance and by praises, he sees the temperament and ambitions of others in their faces and gestures."

## After The Fall

Lorna shunts praises and she just continues to do her good deed without any television fanfare. She has been having Gambia nights collecting materials to take to the villagers since I met her in 1991. As for me, my family and remain grateful to this couple of wingless angels in Colchester.

The Orthopaedic Unit of the proposed hospital of the centre would surely be named after her when in full gear. God bless her and keep her in fit and sound on the opening day ceremonies of the Centre so that villagers would be able to serenade them for their relentless contribution to our dream of providing medical aid to the region and for generations of Gambian villagers.

Finally meet Ghana's sunshine Mrs. Faustina Forkouh. I met this unique lady upon arrival in Manchester last September 2002. Mr. Kinte, a friend and Gambian brother of mine, had arranged that she shelter me for three months while I sort myself out regarding my exams and job feasibility.

It was assumed that my current nightmare would have by then abated. Anyhow she welcomed me with open heart and hands to her abode and refused to charge any fees after hearing my plight. She only said, "I was in serious situation and I am happy to help as much as I can possible cope with it."

## Dr. Alhasan Sidsawo Ceesay, MD

I promised to be a gentleman after she warns that I be good to both of us. As fate would have it took up to end of July 2003 before I can move be on my own. Living with her throughout this elapsed time was lively and very much an education. She and I lived like sister and brother from the same parents.

Faustina is altruist, Ghana's philanthropist and Good Samaritan to all that come seek her help. She would cook and bring food to if she notices that I have had a meal for a day or two. She spends the night awake when my asthma flares I use to feel so guilty putting her through such scary moments.

Simply, she was heaven sent to me for I needed understanding and kindness she showed in accepting to stay at her place until my state improves. When Mustapha Kinte finally reached the "end of his roped" she told him that she would continue to lodge as well as feed me until November 2003 at which time she hopes my difficulties or state would have resolved.

She is the shining star from the Gold Coast that epitomises a typical Ashanti personality. Faustina is gracious, caring and fair when dealing with others.

## After The Fall

I found her warm, friendly and deft indeed. Her friendliness is contagious plus she holds tenaciously onto African culture. Finally, it is said that behind every successful man is the love and managerial effect of a good woman; for me it is these heroines to whom I am profoundly grateful for all the good that happened in my life. They gave their all and dogged their heels so that I succeed in my endeavours for the Gambian villager and humanity.

Mrs. Fatou Koma-Ceesay, Brusubi, Gambia

# Dr. Alhasan Sisawo Ceesay, MD

# Chapter 13

## CHASING TIME TO CATCH A DREAM

It is said that time and tides waits for no man. For me I have been chasing elusive time from time immemorial. The chase started at birth when I stopped breathing in the first hour of my life. In those precious minutes and hours to follow time left me behind and I was declared none existent and was to be buried first thing in the morning.

I woke up before dawn and have been chasing time since February $14^{th}$, 1942 to the present time. My peers in other villages started schooling at the age of 5 years and I started primary school at the raw age of 12 years old. And I enrolled at college at the age of 22 years.

I graduated from medical school at age 50. There has always been this huge gap between time and when things happen for me.

I wish there was a way I can reverse or stop time so that all delays in my life would level up with elapsed time. All my peers have grown grey or have complete white hairs or totally bald but I look like some 28 year old lad and as fit as a 16 years old athletic kid, even though I never ceased chasing after time.

## After The Fall

Time for that precious priceless record of history has not arrived for me. William Shakespeare said of time thus: "Come what comes May. Time and the hour runs through the roughest day." For me it kept flying and irreversibly so. Friends console me by telling me; "Your time will come." In desperation I ask when?

Time cares less for it will tick with or without us. Hence, it is my duty to catch up and do well to live footprints worth following when my time comes. Navigating through the valleys and gorges strewn at us on life's path is a nightmare. I came to England just to do the PLAB and MRCP degree in medicine and return to my home land in the shortest possible time.

This time would not allow as I unknowingly fell into the deepest gorge of visa and job problems. I arrived as a visitor and hence more of tourist than student status. The Home Office's refusal to change my status to student left me in limbo and a destitute.

This made it difficult to pass the PLAB because of being torn between hunger and struggling to find help to send money to feed my equally beleaguered wife and three daughters.

## Dr. Alhasan Sisawo Ceesay, MD

I became catechetic and weak that even the arch angels of death and hell would feel sad and sorry upon meeting me. Again time and tide refused to wait for Dr. Ceesay. All my compatriots got through the PLAB because they had monetary help enabling them to pay for PLAB review courses.

For me I had to feed from the surface of my teeth while I chased time to take my exams under very difficult circumstances that would drown most people. Time was far ahead and I needed to catch up before it becomes too late for me and my dream for the Gambia.

Let me reiterate that the greatest of all faults is to be conscious of none. Hence, time would have not slipped from my fingers had I taken a moment or two to seek for student visa while at the British Embassy in the Gambia. Any how hind sight is always too wise as I later learnt from bitter experience.

Despite this long and hash experience, I never gave up and things happened at a surprising and lightening speed for the arrival of a new dawn in my life and goal for the Gambia.

After The Fall

Chapter 14

THE PARADOXICAL SCHISMS

Back in Africa life is simply or mostly of an agricultural or rural type. It usually starts with education and guidance from parents, initiation, which connotes the day one, is circumcised or inducted into manhood/womanhood, and finally the individual's return to our maker and reunion with our ancestors in the world beyond.

For sojourners like me, it's the beginning of endless challenges and changes we have to adapt to quickly for our survival. Life becomes an endless long hours, 16 or more hours a day, of work with the earning paid to schools, universities, landlords and sending whatever is left to family back in Africa for their sustainers.

It is full of surprises and unfamiliar behaviours, customs, and outcomes. First the weather one encounters unravels in four seasons; spring and summer being the most tolerable but autumn and bone chilling winters are for Eskimos not warm blooded Africans.

Winter curdles my blood and frizzes every bit of me no matter the number of thermal layers I manage to put on.

Dr. Alhasan Sisawo Ceesay, MD

Thanks to technology and kindness of the people over in these frigid places I survived my wintry days in Europe and America. Paradoxically, the expression of freedom and degree to which it is adhered to far exceeded my imagination and expectations.

One of the most surprising paradoxes or schism was being castigated when I attempted to settle a simple dispute between husband and wife friends of mine.

In Africa and most places one can give genuine counsel to warring factors for them to resort to reconciliation instead of being at each other's throat over trivial matters mostly emanating from misunderstanding or failing to listen to the other's point of view.

Let me reiterate what St. Francis of the Franciscan order in Assis, Rome, eloquently admonished us regarding incidence as above. He said, "Where there is discord, May we bring harmony; where is error, may we bring truth, where there is doubt may we bring faith. And where there is despair, may we bring hope."

A dear friend made matters worse for me, by repeatedly asking that I consider moving out of his premises. The demands made on December 5$^{th}$, 2000, May 30$^{th}$, 2001, and again on August 11$^{th}$, 2001were painful experiences.

## After The Fall

However the July 13$^{th}$, 2001 order to relocate from his place was the last straw that made me move. Can you imagine how difficult it was for me to hear that from a friend? I quote, "You have to move any where you can relocate." This brought endless tears of remorse running down my chicks.

It came a year after my wife returned to Gambia living me in solitude and un-employed. There was still no sign of a financial relief by means of acquiring a temporal job until after my being registered with the GMC. Joblessness cum intolerable circumstances catapulted me to Manchester City in the North West region of the UK.

Life did not turn out all roses for me in Manchester. It was a struggle against failures! No pass, No job and no money or peace of mind. My plan to serve as a nurse in UK, until the time I could get my GMC registration, was set a terrible blow when the Overseas Nurses Association stopped processing my request for assistance because the NHS has ceased accepting nurses from regions like mine.

NHS feared draining the health personnel of developing countries by accepting nurse and doctors from underdeveloped countries. What a farce!

## Dr. Alhasan Sisawo Ceesay, MD

In the same vein the very people can go to our countries and shamelessly pick up our gold, diamonds and other mineral wealth without a second thought to poverty their pilfering was doing to the so called developing country.

To make matters worse, if not very grim for me, the Home Secretary announced in April 2006 that from that time hence forth the NHS will only give training priority to UK and EU doctors. Such pronouncements left self-sponsors like me in limbo as we have to fight harder in other to get training placement in teaching hospitals.

This tantamount to a stab from the back from an institute we relied upon. This announcement ignored efforts people like me have been putting in to help improve our medical skills we wish to serve our people back in our countries.

The current state of affairs along with my age nudged me into devoting the rest of my life building Manding Medical Centre to a fully functional health unit serving the Gambia.

After The fall

## Chapter 15

### MANNA NEVER CAME TO ME FROM HEAVEN

I am among few doctors whose life retrograded to the level of living on exactly £5 (five pounds) a week on a nine hours seven days shoe selling job.

The hundred and five pounds weekly earning this slave life brought was split £50 for rent, the other £50 goes towards paying loans I took to pay for my exams, my children's school fees and sustenance of my family back in the Gambia.

Oh! I had a paradoxical raise in salary of £1a day which propped up my income to £16/day. It was disheartening time for me. It was a nightmare neither member of the family will ever forget.

Most painful for me were the times when my daughters ask for shoes or other things their peers have and I had to come out clean and explain that daddy was, even though I would like them have their requests, at no monetary position to provide such items at that time.

I would promise to do my best to get it for them as soon as feasible. I can hear them cry before putting the telephone down or simply passing it to their mother to talk to me.

## Dr. Alhasan Sisawo Ceesay, MD

I do not wish my worst enemy to have to go through such experience or be embedded in hell on earth as my life was. I love my family and missed being with them. Mean while for those who know me, my state was pitiful. Most would ask "Doctor, what on earth are you doing in a shoe shop and not by the patient's bedside?"

I simply reply this is what fate has for me at the moment and I have to feed my family back home. The next day one or two would return to the shop with offering of £2, £5, or £10 for me to send to my children. Yes, I was literally turned out into a silent street beggar and my pride was trampled to the lowest earthly level.

At the end of the day I return to my flat with a heavy heart knowing that I had nothing to eat but two slices of bread with sardine sandwiched in-between. After this kingly meal I try to study for as long as my wondering mind would let me.

The ringing of the telephone brings palpitation and anxiety to me. I fear whether our landlord, back in Gambia, has not gotten impatient with my family or if food has ran out because of uncontrolled daily high prices of food commodities in the Gambia.

## After The Fall

My wife and I use to pray, over the phone, for relief and yet we both know and agreed that life could be worst if I failed my villagers and Manding Medical Centre. So we bit the bullet and continue trying to get more awareness on the good cause Manding medical Centre would bring to the children and villagers.

There are those who think that my enduring such painful experience was predicated on sheer stupidity on my part. For family, especially my wife and I, it was a worthy self-sacrifice for humanity. Life, as ordained, did change for the better and my daughters' education was never set back by the above financial limbo I endured while in the UK.

This is further propounded upon in the following chapter titled, Failure conquered amid roadblocks. Tears do not solve difficult moments like these dark days. Only faith and hard work solves small economic pains as I encountered.

Dr. Alhasan Sisawo Ceesay, MD

## Chapter 16

## Manding Medical Center

When God wants to destroy someone, He first made him an unusual dreamer. So Gandhi had his dream of people solving social deference none violently and Rev. Martin Luther king, jr. held onto his admirable dream of children of Jews and Gentile, black and whites holding hands and living in harmony spearheading peaceful cause for mankind.

There are the Albert Schweitzer's and mother Theresa's of the world dreamers who spent their lives believing in their dreams for mankind. My dream, since 1956, was the simple goal of providing medical aid to those far and in remote villages.

The villager, who is forced to walk miles on end to seek medical aid for his already dying child, wife or friend, deserves a better health system.

Something I saw in 1956 left an indelible mark in my mind and I have since then asked and prayed that God help me bring part if not full to the kind of tragedy that was passing right before me. I was hopelessly unable to give relief except to comfort those involved.

## After The Fall

In 1956, while on my way to Saba village, I met an anxious father carrying his son and his almost dead pregnant wife on the back of donkey heading for the health centre at Kerewan village, three or more miles from where I met him.

The child was vomiting yellow stuff, he was sweaty, his eyes were reverted backwards and the pregnant lady groaning every time the mule moves. There was some greenish fluid dripping off her lapper. She could barely hold the ropes controlling the donkey.

I went to Kerewan later that evening and asked about the status of that family, only to be told that the boy passed away half a mile to the dispensary and the lady was referred to the central hospital in Banjul but the family had no money to pay for her transportation nor was the River ambulance available as it was undergoing maintenance at the Dockyard.

To cut a long story short, both child and mother died because of lack of medical facilities or modern medical aid to the villager. One or all of those lives could have been saved and remain beneficial to the country than the fate that befell them. I prayed and grieved with the family for months and redoubled my efforts at school in other to solve such development in future.

## Dr. Alhasan Sisawo Ceesay, MD

I committed myself to medicine from that day on and never regretted making such a challenging decision in my life. Hence, when on the day I was taking the Hippocratic Oath, I not only swore to uphold all therein but to make sure that God help me not to ever deviate from my commitment and promise to be part of the solution in the health services of the Gambia, to foster health education for the villager, and to complement the existing medical facilities in the Gambia as well as ease the shortage of medical service personnel.

To many, except the dreamer, such path leads to failure as they turn to be white elephants. Some friends tease me by flatly promising to rise from their graves on the opening day of such an Alice in wonderland project. Let me make it crystal clear that I had no illusions about what was needed, or to be done and that the building of the hospital would indeed be a lifetime challenge I am fully ready to grapple with.

There would be a lot of well-wishers but very few will ever want to join until the opening day ceremonies. So first things first, I met an attorney friend Mr. Ousainou Darboe, a villager like me, on September 24, 1992, and pleaded for his assistance with the legal aspects of setting up a charitable foundation, Manding Medical center at Njawara village in the provinces for the sole

## After The Fall

purpose of providing much needed medical aid to the villager. He was very obliging and requested no payment in return for his services. In the mean time I got a board of governors elected while he prepared the memorandum and articles of association of Manding Medical Centre at Njawara village.

Also, I met with the Lower Badibou district chief, Kitabou Singateh, who by the way was my primary school class mate at Kinte Kunda from 1953 to 1957, the District Authority, Commissioner and the kerewan Area Council. All of whom were more than delighted and did all they could under the law to help me set up a grassroots local advisory committee, which was headed by the commissioner, to assist the board and also let the villagers feel being part of the ongoing project.

At my home village, Njawara, a group organized itself and formed a pioneering committee to formally ask the Alkalo (village head/mayor) and the people of Toro Bahen village to donate the earmarked land between it and Njawara for the sole purpose of establishing the Manding Medical Centre on it.

The land issue was partially cleared by the first week of the appeal. In October 1992, Alkalo Omar Koi Bah of Toro Bahen, along with alhaj Musa (Njabi) Bah and Sirimang Bah called my brother, Doudu Ceesay, the elders of Toro

Dr. Alhasan Sisawo Ceesay, MD

Bahen and I to officially inform us that the earmarked land of two plots have been donated to me for the sole purpose of erecting a medical center and hospital facility for the villagers of the region and Gambia. We thanked him for his foresight and kindness towards future generations.

I went back to my lawyer, Ousainu Darboe who by then had finished all work needed for the registration of Manding Medical Centre. We are forever indebted to Alkalos Omar Koi, Arfang Bah, Musa (Njambi) Bah and resident Sirimang Bah, and the people of Toro village. Lastly but not the least our venerable able lawyer Mr. Ousainou Darboe, without whose kindness and legal mind the registration of Manding Medical Centre would have taken longer that it did assisted me.

I also express profound gratitude to the Hon. Chief of Lower Badibou district, Kitabou Singateh, the commissioner, and the local district authority for their understanding and willingness to contribute positively towards our goal and growth. I submitted the registration application material to the Attorney General's Chambers at the Justice Department, Banjul, on October 22, 1992 and Manding Medical Centre was officially registered as an incorporated charitable organization under the companies Act, 1959 by the $27^{th}$ of October 1992.

## After The Fall

Manding Medical Centre' certificate of incorporation is number: 224/1992. With the completion of the paper work and registration of the center, I embarked on a blitz of letter writing informing philanthropists and organizations worldwide about Manding Medical Centre and the need for assistance or donations of medications, equipments, medical videos with which to teach our cadre and villagers to become health worker or evangelist, or nurses and to help us build the center.

To complete the establishment process, after the land was officially ours, I wrote to the following letter to the Ministry of Health informing them of the formation of Manding Medical Centre, a self –help health organization at Njawara, Lower Badibou, North Bank Division, the Gambia. Our temporal address was at 5B Ingram Street in Banjul, capital of the Gambia.

Manding Medical Centre

5B Ingram Street

Banjul, The Gambia

March 2, 1993

Dr. Alhasan Sisawo Ceesay, MD

Permanent Secretary

Ministry of Health

The Quadrangle

Banjul, The Gambia

West Africa


Dear Permanent Secretary

Re: Application for the establishment of a Medical Centre at Njawara in the North Bank.

We are pleased to bring to attention the setting up of a self-help Health organization in the North Bank Division at Njawara village.

The directorates and members of the organization would be more than grateful if the Ministry of Health would allow us establish Manding Medical Centre at Njawara village, Lower Badibou District of the Gambia.

Manding Medical Centre, when fully operational, will provide medical, surgical, gynaecology and obstetrics, Paediatrics and other facilities to the villagers. It will also help ease the shortage of medical facilities in that region.

Dr. Alhasan Sisawo Ceesay, MD

Manding Medical Centre will have health education secessions in the villages as an effort to enlighten our youths. Again, thank you for taking time to consider our application and we certainly look forward to a positive recognition of the need for such a center in the rural sector of the Gambia.

I am anxiously waiting to hear from your office at your convenience. Regards

Yours sincerely

Dr. Alhasan S. Ceesay, MD

Director/Coordinator

Meanwhile the villagers grew more enthused and throngs of them attended our monthly health field trips or clinics. The attendance grew so large that we ended up listing the villages to attend in turn of nine villages per trip. This usually totals to a bit above 1,000 patients at a given visit.

I normally go on weekends with three doctors and at times four volunteer doctors along with Nurses aid Mrs. Mbee Sonko and Ida Njie to assist us do the job. The field trips/clinics start with an announcement by Radio Gambia giving the names of villages expected to attend and at which village health center.

## After The Fall

The clinic day starts with an early morning breakfast by the team and then a ride to the village health center where we would find the villagers and their sick ones assembled. Every occasion starts with the offering of prayers and then the various village heads, in attendance help us in organizing the flow of people wanting to be seen by one of our team doctors.

In most cases the day goes trouble free but at certain localities the political tension does make it very difficult to have such large groups of people without little arguments. Thanks to the Commissioner (s) for deploying the police or making them available to quell trouble and help us maintain order during these clinics. Commissioner Lamin Koma can tell you how rough things can be at some of these clinic centers. He was trapped in one of these bad moments of people rushing to be in the front line of the queue to see one our doctors. The Ministry of Health finally sent us the following affirmative reply as thus: -

Ministry of Health & Social services

The Quadrangle

Banjul, The Gambia

Dr. Alhasan Sisawo Ceesay, MD

Ref.P510/289/01(95)

Dr. Alhasan Ceesay

Manding Medical Centre

5B Ingram Street

Banjul, The Gambia

Dear Dr. Ceesay,

RE: Application to establish a Medical Centre at Njawara

I acknowledge receipt of your letter of the $2^{nd}$ March 1993 on the above-mentioned subject. I wish to inform you that this Ministry has no objection to your application to establish Manding Medical Centre at Njawara.

This initiative is in line with our national health policies and we would render our support in our joint efforts to improve the health of the people.

Signed: N. Ceesay

For Permanent Secretary

## After The Fall

After several more field trips it was suggested we apply for a None Governmental Organization (NGO) status. It was believed that if we become and NGO, help would come our way quicker.

I went to work on this suggestion and arranged for Tango Secretariat Centre to send one of the United Nations voluntary program officers to come and evaluate our performance relative to the objectives of Manding Medical Centre.

This was accepted and a field trip was set up for September 12 to 22, 1995. Radio Gambia made the announcement well ahead of the time for our arrival and the following was the outcome of that august gathering of September 21 &22, 1995.

Dr. Alhasan Sisawo Ceesay, MD

Alagie Mama at Njawara primary School

# After The Fall

## Chapter 17

TANGO SECRETARIAT TRIP REPORT ON MANDING MEDICAL CENTRE, SEPTEMBER 21 – 22, 1995

A field trip to Kerewan at the North Bank Division was organized by the Manding Medical Centre Executive Director Dr. Alhasan S. Ceesay in conjunction with Tango Secretariat Centre to see the organization's activities and meet the members before recommending the organization as a member of Tango.

On September 21, 1995, two meetings were organized in two big centers where members gather to air their views and experience from the organization. Alkalos, chiefs, imams, women, men and youths attended these meetings.

The key leadership from five villages in their speeches showed interest and support for the project and organization. Alkalo of Toro Bahen Omar Koi and chiefs donated the land for the constructing of Manding Medical Centre, the hospital and its ancillaries. The two meeting were highly attended and successful.

Dr. Alhasan Sisawo Ceesay, MD

The Tango (UNV) program officer Mr. Muloshi on behalf of Tango gave a keynote speech on Tango's operations and activities as an umbrella organization and urged members to work hand in hand with the organization in their efforts to develop their villages and North Bank area.

The three meetings with the commissioner during the field trip on our courtesy call were successful and encouraged the executive Director of Manding Medical Centre, Dr. Alhasan Ceesay, to cooperate with the strict, especially the commissioner who is one of the advisors in the local committee.

The commissioner thanked Tango for making the purpose of the mission clear to him and promised that he will try by all means to cooperate with Tango in the area of Technical advice and institution capacity building. Clinic day was organized on September 22, 1995 at Njawara and 150 people attended and got treatments.

RECOMMENDATION

Looking at the calibre of leadership and development activities compared to some NGO tango members in comparison to Manding Medical Centre, the organization need consideration since they have already activities with a promising future.

## After The Fall

Looking at the composition of the Board, they have people with a great vision. They have strong membership and backup at the grassroots levels. The organization has chosen to do what is right at the right time and their concentration in one area is vital and a good starting point.

Any success achieved by any organization depended on good leadership and discipline. Manding Medical Centre has quality leadership and deserves NGO status.

Signed: M. Muloshi

UNV Program Officer

We were delighted by the recommendation made by the United Nations voluntary Program Officer in the Gambia. We redoubled our efforts to contact organizations seeking help worldwide.

In between letters and monthly field trips to different select health centers we were blessed with visits from interested friends and groups or representatives of similar organizations in the globe. I had several telephone calls to Dr. Edward Brown, an official of the World Bank in Washington, D. C. responsible of the bank's health affairs at the time.

Dr. Alhasan Sisawo Ceesay, MD

He was very receptive and had several added discussions with Dentist Melvin George, then Director of Medical and Health Service for the Gambia, on how the bank could help in the financing of the building of Manding Medical Centre.

These talks went on well and Dr. Edward brown gave me his promise and personal commitment to helping the project and that we have to start in a small scale and the building will have to be done in several well planned phases.

Dr. Sidi C. Jammeh, a former Armitage School colleague, promised to help me by constantly reminding Dr. Brown of the need to help us with the project. This kept the momentum at the World Bank alive for Manding Medical Centre.

Among our guest were a couple from Colchester, Essex, UK, Lorna V. Robinson and husband Keith Robinson were very impressed by our project and enthusiasm of the ordinary villagers about Manding Medical Centre.

They fell in love with the idea and objectives of the self-help health organization and promised to help as much as they could. We had by this time submitted application for NGO status and ACCNO Secretary replied thus:

After The Fall

ACCNO Secretariat

Dept. of Community Development

13 Mariner Parade

Babjul, The Gambia

September 12, 1994

Ref.CD/ACCNO/Vol3/(183)

Dr. Alhasan S. Ceesay

Director/Coordinator

Manding Medical Centre

P. O. Box 640

Banjul, The Gambia

Dear Sir,

RE: application for an NGO status within the ACCNO framework

Dr. Alhasan Sisawo Ceesay, MD

Please find enclosed a self-explanatory letter from the Ministry for local government and lands concerning the approval of your application for NGO status. ACCCNO Secretariat congratulates your organization for successfully completing the registration process and wishes you a fruitful relationship in the field of development.

Thank you for your cooperation

Yours Faithfully

Musu Ngujo

For: ACCNO desk Officer

Cc: file & R/File

Replies from our worldwide appeal letters did not pour in money nor did they materialized beyond promises to help in due course. Hence, I decided to open up a pharmacy at my expense at my residence in the Bundung area of Serekunda using the proceeds from its sales to finance the health field trips and activities of the organization. This meant spending an extra three to four at the pharmacy daily after eight hours at the RVH before rejoining my family.

## After The Fall

All drugs used for the treatment of patients at our field trip clinics were purchased from sales I made at the Bundung Pharmacy. A local agency, known as IBAS, lent me D8000, interest free, which was used in buying drugs and paying for transportation for the project's activities. The loan was completely repaid well ahead of the allowed sixteen months period given by IBAS.

We are obliged and grateful to Aja Ndey Oley Jobe and management of IBAS for their kindness to assist us at the time. Just when things were about to be financially complete for us to start the first phase of building the various sections of the hospital, came the unexpected coup d'etat of July 22, 1994. The reaction from would be our donors and supporters or sponsors were swift and equally unexpected.

All those who were considering giving the project a chance sited likelihood of sudden national unrest and instability as reasons for their withdrawal of promised aid and participation while some suggested my waiting until after the transition phase of the coup d'etat before they would reconsider reopening our files with them.

## Dr. Alhasan Sisawo Ceesay, MD

Again it resorted to legend or case of the chicken the egg, which came first as no one, knew when the transition would end and we kept our fingers crossed hoping that daylight will be ours in not far distance.

It was a severe blow to our hope and for getting the type of interest and support that was engendered for Manding Medical Centre would be difficult to match after such crisis that occurred in the Gambia.

Many were acting in conjunction with their governments, which were not sure of what the future under military rule would be for the Gambia. All prospective and possible international sources earmarked for Manding Medical Centre were either frozen or evaporated into thin air with the coup leaving me floating in the middle of the ocean of despair without a life jacket except God's merciful hands.

I knew the villagers would grow restless if nothing happens in the direction of building the center. I called an emergency general meeting with members from most of the villages and told them of the new challenge and development and this information not only fell on deaf ears but left their spirits dampened.

## After The Fall

Interest waxed and waned at some quarters but I kept on trying my best not to be despondent like the others have shown. I kept the organization alive under very limited funds raised from the pharmacy at Bundung until my trip to the UK in January 2000.

Before leaving the Gambia, the Commissioner for north Bank Division and chairman of the local advisory committee for Manding Medical Centre, Mr. Lamin Koma, gave me the following letter to assist me in my fund raising drive while in England and possible other European countries. It read thus:

The Commissioner

Kerewan Village

North Bank Division

The Gambia, West Africa

June 15, 1998

TO WHOM IT MAY CONCERN

I hereby write to testify and confirm that Manding Medical Centre is a self-help health project situated at Njawara village, North Bank Division.

Dr. Alhasan Sisawo Ceesay, MD

As the Commissioner of this division I was elected as the Chairman of the local advisory Committee of the Manding Medical Centre. As I am concerned, I am aware of this self-help project since it took off the ground, by the able hands of Dr. Alhasan S. Ceesay, a born citizen of Njawara village.

The purpose of the establishing of such a medical centre is to provide medical attention/care to all Gambians irrespective of religion, tribe, nationality or gender and age within the country and sub-region.

It is in these regards that this office writes to seek for your assistance in providing support in cash/kind to make this medical center a reality. I look forward to your continued support and cooperation.

Signed: V. Baldeh

For Commissioner

North Bank Division

The new millennium started with good omen for Manding Medical Centre. I have been invited to go to Europe and America on a fund raising trip for the center but could not because of my commitment with the Royal Victoria Hospital (RVH). I needed a longer vacation period to be able to travel and keep my job at the same time.

## After The Fall

Above all my family needed the monetary support, which would fade away if I lost the post at the RVH. Hence, to my delight and greatest timely occurrence I heard from my long-standing friend in Colchester, Mrs. Lorna V. Robinson, inviting my wife and I to come to the UK to attend the wedding of their younger daughter on January $9^{th}$, 2000.

Coincidentally, I had just started my annual leave, which was to finish on the $26^{th}$ of January 2000. The excitement mounted when we received a fax from the visa officer at the British High Commission in the Gambia requesting that we report to the visa processing office with our passports on Tuesday 8.30 am January $4^{th}$, 2000 for processing of our visas for our pending travels to the UK.

This took me by surprise because of the casual way we had discussed the possibility of such a trip. So when we got the telephone call followed by the said fax from the visa section I was caught off guard and had to rush through all the preparations for my wife and I to travel to UK without a second thought on whether adequate arrangements were being made for my eventual pursuit of a postgraduate degree (MRCP) in internal medicine.

Dr. Alhasan Sisawo Ceesay, MD

Hind side has it that I needed to discuss this aspect with the visa councillor and request for eventual student visa status or leave to remain until my completion of the post graduate degree I wanted to pursue.

Miss Famatanding Ceesay, Daughter

## After The Fall

God's ways and timing are best for every occasion. I was yearning to get a way out of the financial limbo the center ran into since the change of government in the Gambia. Now that opportunity was suddenly thrown on my laps by Lorna Robinson's open-ended invitation for my wife and to attend their daughter's wedding ceremony in the UK.

Interested donors started being weary about Military rule and possible restlessness that may ensue. Hence, Manding Medical Centre literally lost all its prospective overseas support as well as sponsors most of who had cold feet after the July coup d'etat of 2004.

I ended up running the center from my meagre salary of D1500 or seventy-five pounds sterling per month and of literally hard labour with long hours at a time. The other source was from what little I could make from sales at the Bundung pharmacy.

To cut a long story short we were granted visas to travel to the UK. We left the Gambia on the 6$^{th}$ of January 2000 on a new footing and challenge to bring back some life into Manding Medical center while in England. I got on the ball as soon as the wedding ceremony was over. I obtained a three–year study leave from the Management Board of the Royal Victoria Hospital in Banjul.

Dr. Alhasan Sisawo Ceesay, MD

This gave me all the time I needed to try to rekindle interest in the center and thereby inject into Manding Medical center cash flow it needed to help us meet or our targeted goal and objective for the farming community in the North Bank Division of the Gambia. It was more like a miracle entering this new concrete and direct ways.

Help from my host Lorna Robinson of Colchester, Essex, UK further anointed my hands. Lorna and I wrote several letters to various places, including celebrities and organizations, most of who replied in the negative because of perception they had about the political climate in Gambia since the coup d'etat of July $22^{nd}$ 1994.

Nonetheless some hinted being interested at a later date, meaning when the solders return to camp. A few donated small amounts plus hospital items. By now it became clear that we have to counter the perception most, on this side of the isles feel or had about the Gambia at the time.

This dreadful start did not alarm me much for I am fully aware of the wrong information about the average African in the village, who like most, is just a decent human being trying to earn an honest living for himself, family and community.

## After The Fall

Villagers are least interested in all the political gimmickry shrouding and clothing their lives. I do not at all blame the rest of world for getting sick and tired of helping and not seeing any tangible good come out of it and worse some African politicians and regimes show no interest in helping move the African people onto better and modern rewarding modalities of life.

They offer more lip service than opening avenues for progress. How many knew that the Ethiopian starvation was politically orchestrated by the previous Mangestu regime? Genocide regime and the heartlessness of some African politicians made me feel sick.

To remove any possible sceptics regarding Manding Medical Centre and its objectives we decided to have it registered as a charitable organization in the UK under the name of Colchester Friends of Manding charitable trust.

The Robinson knew a solicitor who would be so kind to help us with the legal aspect of the registration process with UK charity Commission. They spoke to Mr. Bruce Ballard of the Birkett long Solicitors to come to our aid. This kind gentleman, like my lawyer friend, Mr. Ousainou Darboe, gladly agreed to help and sent us a draft of the Trust deed.

## Dr. Alhasan Sisawo Ceesay, MD

After a series of changes were made on the draft he forwarded our request to be registered in the UK as a charitable organization helping its twin partner or parent group, Manding Medical Centre at Njawara village in the Gambia, West Africa.

Meanwhile, we concentrated our activities through media campaign effort to call attention to existence of Friends of Manding and their desire in building a hospital for Manding Medical Centre at Njawara, the Gambia. Again we ran into a very gentle heart in the person of Miss Helen Anderson of Colchester who was the Community website editor for Essex County.

She went head over heels regarding the idea of helping others so far away when approached by Lorna Robinson. Helen thought the idea wonderful and at the same time helped us have our own website and also had an article published by the Evening Gazette which had a large reader circulation.

In the same vein I got the interest of Dr. Linda Mahon-Daly, Dr. Peter Wilson, Dr. Laurel Spooner, Dr. Richard Spooner, Dr. Philip Murray, Dr. Barbara Murray, Dr. Fredric Payne, who by the way was our Medical superintendent under who I worked at the RVH during the later part of colonial Gambia, along with many surgeries in the Colchester area.

## After The Fall

These were my Good Samaritans of the day who worked acidulously to make Manding Medical Centre become a reality for the villagers in the Gambia. Dr. Linda Mahon-Daly helped distribute letters about Manding Medical Centre to nearly all her colleagues in the Colchester Borough and so did Dr. Laurel Spooner.

Bless their hearts for kindness and job well done. The news article published by the Evening Gazette brought us another very helpful and kind person, Mr. Malkait Singh who is an ophthalmologist and had made several trips to the Gambia before knowing about the Friends of Manding.

He was delighted to join Neville Thompson, Connie Thompson, Lorna Robinson, Keith Robinson, Loenard Thompson, Mark Naylor, Barbara Philips and others as pioneering members of Friends of Manding. Mr. Malkait Singh and I grew to be very good friends and he had since given me lots of personal monetary help to cater for my exams and family back in the Gambia.

I am very grateful for interest and kindness, and concern he showed about my family. A few months after the formation of Friends of Manding, Dr. Laurel Spooner spent a week in the Gambia vacationing and doing some fact finding about the center.

Dr. Alhasan Sisawo Ceesay, MD

During which time she visited Manding Medical Centre at Njawara in the North Bank Division. The villagers were happy to meet her and thanked her about good work being done in Colchester regarding Manding Medical Centre.

Everyone was happy about the news that people in the UK were poised to assist Manding Medical Centre goes forward in its drive to provide medical aid to villagers. A meeting of member of the Friends of Manding was scheduled for the first week of February 2001.

Mean while our solicitor continued pressing for registration of Friends of Manding, which is the arm and Manding Medical Centre's Colchester branch support group, as charity in the UK.

Dr. Laurel Spooner suggested we start with small-scale form of the center and then gradually expand as funds become available. This consideration would be studied in full and deliberated upon by the committee during the forth-coming February meeting.

After The Fall

Keith, Dr. Ceesay, and Mrs. Lorna Robinson

Dr. Alhasan Sisawo Ceesay, MD

Miss Binta Ceesay, Daughter

After The Fall

Chapter 18

## WHAT IS MANDING MEDICAL CENTRE?

Manding Medical Centre, located at Njawara village in the North Bank Region, Gambia, West Africa, is a self-help village health organization founded by Dr. Alhasan S. Ceesay.

Its objective is to provide medical service to the villagers by providing efficient and affordable medical aid to all people in and around the Gambia, especially the rural sector.

We are dedicated to relieving suffering and ensure effective treatment for villagers and all attending Manding Medical Centre at Njawara, NBR.

ESTABLISHED

The Manding Medical Centre is founded by Dr. Alhasan Sisawo Ceesay, a native of Njawara village in 1992, because of sheer shortage of medical service to the region and the preponderance of premature deaths by children from Malaria, malnutrition, diarrhoea, and worm infestations.

These childhood maladies account for almost 25% of Gambian children's death before the age of five years.

Dr. Algasan Sisawo Ceesay, MD

The Gambia Ministry of Health officially recognized the Centre in 1995 and prior to which it became a None Governmental Organization (NGO) on September 12th, 1994. In addition, the Manding Medical Centre now has Friends of Manding Charitable Trust, Colchester, Essex, UK as its arm and liaison in the UK and the European Union countries.

The Friends of Manding is a registered charity in England and Wales. Its registration number is 1088136 since August 21, 2001. In similar development and purpose, Dr. Avery Aten heads the Friends of Manding Alpena Charitable Trust, Alpena, Michigan, UAS since May 2005.

MISSION STATEMENT

Suffering in another human being is a call to the rest of us to stand in fellowship. It requires us to be there and it is a mystery, which demands the spirit of caring, sharing and our presence. Our duty as healthcare professionals is providing medical care, which is a fundamental right of all human beings.

This village health organization is dedicated to providing medical aid to the rural sector and farming community in the Gambia. It will compliment the health service in the Gambia in addition it will promote preventive medicine in the hinterland of the Gambia.

## After The Fall

MEMBERSHIP

Well over twenty thousand villagers, comprising of farmers, village heads, and chiefs, the Kerewan Area Council, Commissioners and local District Authority are now fully active enthusiastic members of Manding Medical Centre.

All are welcomed to join the endeavours of the centre. People from the rest of the globe are more than welcomed to participate or share with us our dream in bring much needed medical service to people in desperate state because of lack of medical facilities.

ACTIVITIES

Manding Medical Centre tries to alleviate some of the above mentioned health problems and situations by having bimonthly health field trips/clinics to villages teaching them about health, preventive medicine and hygiene that would help reduce the number infected and the vectors responsible for these diseases.

We encourage antenatal and postnatal attendance of clinics by mothers and we treat the sick amongst them with minimum charge to not so elderly and pregnant young ladies.

Dr. Alhasan Sisawo Ceesay, MD

The service is free to children, the very elderly, and the indigent needing emergency treatment. The rest pay amounts well below tat in private practice.

Money accrued is subsequently used to buy drugs with which to treat the patients and for other projects of the center. When in cession the center treats well more than 1000 patients per field trip to the villages.

We provide free information and advisory service on aids and sexually transmitted diseases (STDs) to the young, all patients, their relatives and friends. We also plan to have a Nursing School in due course to augment not only staff but also the government health centers when the need arises.

IMMEDIATE GOAL AND APPEAL

The villagers are very enthused about the center and Toro Bahen village, next to Njawara village, has donated two plots of land for the building of the center and its ancillary units, which is now leased to manding medical center for ninety-nine years.

More than 2000 children die tragically from malaria and other childhood ailments stated above for shortage of health services.

## After The Fall

We are eager to start building the children' and maternity wings of the proposed Gambia General Hospital at Manding Medical Centre and do need raise the required 900,000 pounds sterling to accomplish our goal.

Ten bags of cement cost thirty pounds sterling or $60 (sixty us dollars). Also we would be most grateful if we could be assisted with medicines and equipment to facilitate our work.

Hence we implore you to kindly support our yearning to build the children' and maternity wings of Manding Medical Centre. We are dedicated to providing medical aid to the villager, especially children. We are investors in people and you are invited to join the endeavors of Manding Medical Centre at Njawara village, the Gambia, West Africa.

Help us make a difference and beacon of hope for the villagers. Please give generously. Today's hope can be tomorrow's reality. We want to contribute positively towards the health services of the Gambia, and with this center in place it will create greater health awareness and privation by the villagers. Cash contributions of any amount should be sent in the name of Manding Medical Centre, to the Friends of Manding charitable Trust, 82 Finchingfield Way, Blackheath, Colchester, Essex, CO2 OAU, and England.

## Dr. Alhasan Sisawo Ceesay, MD

It is vital to be certain that Dr. Alhasan S. Ceesay is informed of your contribution via email thus: alhasanceesay@hotmail.co.uk. Your kindness and humane consideration to help save lives will always be deeply appreciated and grateful for by the villagers, the Gambia and I.

OVERSEASES LINKS

The Friends of Manding in Colchester, Essex County, UK, is formed by a local group of residents, doctors, and nurses who regularly visited the Gambia and is in support of Manding Medical Centre. Manding medical center through the auspices of the Friends of Manding recently received recognition and registration by the UK Charity Commission.

They serve as support and our liaison in the Europe Union. The Friends of Manding in behalf of Manding Medical Centre at Njawara has been entered in the central Register of charities with effect from August 21, 2001; the registration number is 1088136 for England and Wales.

Also, a similar charitable trust, the Alpena Friends of Manding Charitable Trust of Michigan, USA, has been established in Alpena, Michigan in June 2006.

## After The Fall

It's headed by Dr. Avery Aten a resident physician chairman of the Women and newborn of the Alpena region Community Health along with the medical community of Alpena.

Ntoro Bahen village, Badibou, NBR, The Gambia

Dr. Alhasan Sisawi Ceesay, MD

Chapter 19

MANDING MEDICAL CENTRE MILESTONES

Manding Medical Centre has been in my mind's drawing board since the early 1950s but it took off in earnest when I returned to the Gambia, after graduating from medical school in 1992. The Centre is registered as a charity with the Attorney general's Office, Department of Justice, Banjul, The Gambia, since 1993.

The Gambia Ministry of Health also recognized it in the same year. Toro Bahen village, Lower Badibou, NBD, Gambia, donated two huge plots of land for the location of the center in 1993. Our none governmental (NGO) status was approved in 1994.

On September 21, 1995 Tango Secretariat sent a United Nations voluntary program Officer, Mr. Muloshi on field trip to evaluate the organizational and extent of support for Manding Medical Centre at Njawara village.

Mr. Muloshi's recommendation after two days field trip to the region stated thus; "Looking at the caliber of leadership and development activities to some NGO Tango members in comparison to Manding Medical Centre, the organization need consideration since they have already activities with a promising future.

After The Fall

Looking at composition of the Board, they have people with a vision. They have strong membership and backup at grass root levels. The organization has chosen to what is right at the right time and their concentration in one area is vital and good starting point.

Any success achieved by any group or organization depends on good leadership and discipline. Manding Medical Centre has high quality leadership and deserves NGO status." It was not until my travels to the UK in 2000 that the Friends of Manding Charitable Trust was formed and registered as charity in England and Wales by the UK Charity Commission.

Friends of Manding is the extended arm of Manding Medical Centre at Njawara, The Gambia. They serve as our liaison in the UK and the European Union. Please browse on our website thus: http://friendsofmandinggambimed.btck.co.uk, to learn more or for further information about our work and organization.

We are still on fund raising activities to earn enough to enable us build the children' and maternity units of the hospital at Manding Medical Centre at Njawara. In May 2005, 11 American students and their instructor Mr. Thomas Ray visited Manding Medical Centre at Njawara.

Dr. Alhasan Sisawo Ceesay, MD

Additionally, input from has now resulted in Alpena City, Michigan, USA, twining by proclamation with Njawara and Kinte kunda villages in Gambia respectively on the 5$^{th}$ of December 2005.

In June 2006, Dr. Avery Aten, Chairman of the Women and Newborn of Alpena Region Health Community along with the medical community of Alpena commenced processing application for a charitable Trust to be named Alpena friends of Manding Charitable Trust, Michigan, USA.

This will soon be finalized and up and running to help Dr. Alhasan Ceesay in the provision of medicine and educational assistance to schools in the Lower Badibou district, the Gambia, West Africa.

In August 2008, Dr. Alhasan Ceesay and the Badibou Cultural Dance Troupe will visit Alpena and other cities in Michigan for fund raising drive to enable the building of the Manding Medical Centre children and maternity units at Njawara village.

Dr. Richard Bates, an Obyng, and a number of medical professionals involved in obstetrics and gynecology at Alpena, Michigan joined Manding Medical Centre's crusade on 17/08/07.

After The Fall

Chapter 20

TEMPLATE FOR REGIONAL DEVELOPMENT

Manding Medical Centre became a template for districts elsewhere and villagers to nurture, develop further and handover to the next generation. This None Governmental Health Organization epitomizes a developmental watchtower for the region.

Manding medical center is a pulsating source of hope, jobs training and superb medical service at Njawara village the Gambia. Everyone knows that government alone does not move things fast enough. Society must be radical and pragmatic to pitch into its development.

We know all too well that the developed world got where it is because private efforts were self prophetic and projects like Manding Medical Centre goes long ways to initiate and stimulate community to work together for a positive agenda for its people.

Hence after many years of foot dragging and vicissitude by society I decided I will build the hospital if I have to single-handed. I worked years receiving no government assistance and without grants from the great of the Gambian community.

## Dr. Alhasan Sisawo Ceesay, MD

Manding Medical Centre is a positive good that help our regions to cross the road to a better healthcare delivery. We thank everyone for making it possible that our center became a platform and guide in rejuvenating our regions.

We now provide medical service to all Gambians and none Gambians domiciled in the Gambia. We will create more jobs as need arises. This was the reason why I gave my life's comfort for reward that will benefit most needy villagers.

It came through determination and kindness of many people worldwide. There are some things only governments can do but together communities through collective initiatives can achieve at least fifty percent of their developmental needs in addition to government effort.

Today some see Manding medical centre as perpetual monument of good, an honour to the country and a general benefit to villagers and children in the North Bank of the Gambia. Manding medical centre is an inspiration and cause for thankfulness and celebration.

# After The Fall

Miss Roheyata Ceesay, Daughter

Dr. Alhasan Sisawo Ceesay, MD

Chapter 21

AN APPEAL TO INTERNATIONAL COMMUNITY

Dear Readers,

The above information about Manding Medical Centre is included in this work only hoping that it will help spread the word more extensively and draw awareness to a greater community of people and readers of my work.

It is my belief that lots of good people out there may want to participate or give to the cause and goal of the center should they be aware of its existents for the villagers. Hence, I am appealing for help and participatory support from all able to extend their hearts to make this much needed medical endeavour to come to fruition for the rural sector of the Gambia.

Who knows you might even end up coming to bask in our beautiful seaside and relish Gambian generosity. Music for me is reaching out to help others and my patients are yearning for your kind participation and donation in cash/kind. Thanks a million for considering our appeal. God blesses your heart(s). I write with believe that by it money can be generated to provide a much needed medical service to the rural sector. Writing about the Manding Medical Centre may course some Good Samaritan and any wanting to leave foot prints on the

## After The Fall

sand of time for a good cause to come to our assistance to help us meet the goals of the center at Njawara village, the Gambia, West Africa. My head, heart and soul are devoted to my family, the Gambia and Manding Medical Centre. It is not a God given calling but a mere conviction that our rural folks deserve better health service than currently available and hence human calling to want to contribute positively to bring resolution of some of our rural health service inadequacies.

I never had an angel come down to me nor have I ever heard the voices of God saying, "Ceesay, you must do so and so" as many mocked Manding Medical Centre emanated from sheer conviction that it is a dutiful way of doing the right thing for curbing premature deaths of children before reaching 5 years of life from malaria, water born diseases, and warm infestations; and in the same vein providing both pre and postnatal care to the pregnant.

Hence, portions of proceeds of sales in all my work go to help meet the center's operational costs and in providing scholarship to indigent indigenous rural candidates due course return to serve rural Gambia wishing to read for a medical degree or agriculture and Medicine.

Signed: Dr. Alhasan S. Ceesay, MD/Email: alhasanceesay@hotmail.com

# Dr. Alhasan Sisawo Ceesay, MD

## Chapter 22

### LORNA ROBINSON, AN ANGEL OF MERCY

Keith, Dr. Ceesay, and Lorna Robinson(RIP)

## After the fall

There are certain moulds God broke them moments after He finished making them. Mrs. Lorna V. Robinson was one of these unique, caring, sharing and rare angels of mercy.

Mrs. Lorna Robinson and I met through her job as general nurse at the then Essex County General hospital in Colchester, Essex County in 1990, when I was a trainee doctor at the hospital.

She and husband Keith Robinson became my friends as far back as in the 1990s and one of their annual pilgrimages is visiting my family in the Gambia, West Africa.

This benevolent couple has since been my Colchester if not my England. Together we set to catch a dream of providing medical aid and service to Gambian villagers. I left at the end of my training to serve my country in 1992. In December 1999 Mrs. Lorna Robinson sent an invitation for my wife and I to attend wedding of Miss Fiona Robinson, her younger daughter, to gentleman Reeves.

We have since 2000 worked acidulously to make the above goal come to fruition, especially for those in the rural sector of the North Bank Region of the Gambia. It was Lorna's joint effort with, nurses, Doctors Laurel

Spooner, Barbara Murray, Richard Spooner, Phil Murray, Linda Mahon-Daly, Peter R. Wilson, Malkait Singh and residents of Colchester, which lead to the formation of the Colchester Friends of Manding Charitable Trust.

It was registered as a charity in England and Wales in 2001. The charity number is 1088136. This charity acts as liaison in the European Union countries for Manding Medical Centre at Njawara village in the Badibous of the North Bank Region, the Gambia.

Since its conception, the Friends of Manding Charitable Trust had busied itself on weekly or bimonthly Gambibarzaars in an effort to help raise money for building of both the children and maternity units of the center.

Mrs. Lorna Robinson spent countless week-ends either selling material such as toys, coats and anything she could lay her hands on as long as she believes it will generate money for the building of the children and maternity units of the center.

She spent most of her retirement time organizing activity for the center to help promote our cause. She sent books, spectacles, pens and pencils along with medication for the center's use.

The influence of this Good Samaritan group in Colchester reverberated and lead to the formation of a similar charity group in America, which is lead by Dr. Avery Aten,

Dr. Alhasan Sisawo Ceesay, MD

Alpena Friends of Manding Charitable Trust, Michigan, USA, was formed in May 2005. All this came about because Mrs. Lorna V. Robinson, the lady of mercy behind the wheel, would not rest while the indigent goes without the most basic things in life.

Here is how Lorna views her part during one of many conversations we had about the need to share worth and ourselves with other less fortunate than us.

She simply said, "Ceesay, I feel delighted and warm at heart in helping others, like the villagers. I strongly belief good used could be made from my work and experience I had at the NHS over years.

I will try to recruit as many retired nurses to our cadre as long as they listen to my please. The other secrete is that such activity keeps me young, participating and contributing to the needy. I feel alive and forever growing. In life we most extend our hearts to others and with compassion reach the needy."

This tit bit tells about the unselfish nature of Mrs. Lorna V. Robinson who through the years since her retirement gave her all to help others, especially the villagers, breathe a sigh of relief and to have hope and knowledge that someone far away they never met cared about them.

## After the fall

Lorna continued saying, "It brings joy to my heart when I share the little I have with the needy. It helps to uplift the despondent. Millions suffer needlessly for not having means of proper health care, clean and safe water, good shelter and chance to attend schools.

I want to help you get the villagers from a downward spiral of deepening health deprivation. I certainly take hope in people like you and your stand to help your folks back home in the Gambia."

It was this unique caring angel that I lost on the third of March 2010 for she returned peacefully to her maker on this day. The above was my Lorna and now I cry, when shall we be blessed will another like her?

Losing Lorna Robinson left me feeling that I lost the best person, outside of my family, I ever known. She was a kind soul of unswerving determination to share the little She had with the little guy needing her help. She stood by my cause in thick and thin moments of my stay in the United Kingdom.

Dr. Alhasan Sisawo Ceesay, MD

Dr. Alhasan S. Ceesay graduating from the American University of the Caribbean, West Indies, 1992

## After The Fall

The provision of medical care to villagers is more than a responsibility; it is a sacred trust for me. I will not the villagers or memory Mrs. Lorna V. Robinson down because I believe in looking to the well being of the less fortunate. One carries on trying on reflecting on all the children and villagers who need this health care. Hence no trepidation will hold me back.

My family, the villagers and I miss and deeply mourn her premature departure from mother earth. May she rest in peace with her maker and may we the living without fail or fear able to follow the high shining examples of indefatigable Good Samaritan she was in life.

I hope you will join me to keep her memory and legacy alive for other to copy while we continue taking medical aid to villagers in rural Gambia. Lorna V. Robinson thanks a million and goodbye for now.

Signed: Dr. Alhasan S. Ceesay, MD

Manding Medical Centre, Njawara

The Gambia, West Africa. E-mail: alhasanceesay@hotmail.com

Dr. Alhasan Sisawo Ceesay, MD

## Chapter 23

### MY SAMARITAN MEN OF GOOD WILL

Every successful person had Samaritan angels who Offered their shoulders for him or her to stand on and see further than most. Compiled herein are my Samaritan men of goodwill.

Hence, I beg leave to indulge in a bit of sentimentality about a few rare human angels who played major part in today's success and help for my villagers. Believe me their moulds, as you will soon find, are beyond those of simple people.

These men help me reach today's pedestal. In medicine for the villager, I profiled ladies who championed my cause. Now, bear with me for just a few lines on the Samaritan men of goodwill.

They like the previously mentioned ladies al not only believe in my dream and objective for the villager but also gave all they could to help make that dream come to fruition.

These men gave unparalleled needed help and friendship to me when I was distressed and in utter despair and darkness. Some even shed a few tears with me because the pain and set back certain roadblocks caused my goal.

## After The Fall

One of these was the day I received GMC' e-mail of the 17$^{th}$ June 2008 recanting recognition of my primary medical qualification based on frivolous website enter. Hell brewed to its hottest temperatures, as it took time to unravel the misunderstanding, before GMC rectified the error.

However, with your indulgence let us start from the beginning of the geneses. It was with God' anointing hand in conjunction with Sisawo Bajo Ceesay, alias Sisawo Salah) that my twin partner I landed on this Garden of Eden. Father gave us love and good guidance throughout his life with us. He and I had deferent perception about western Education and culture but we reconciled after my completing primary school at Kinte Kunda.

My father's experience from the hands of colonials made him never to entertain idea of his progeny deviating from the farmers' mould. Nor would he allow me pursue Western Education and ideology, which at the time was alien to my father and his peers.

He once told me: "Son, my wish for you is to be a hard working good farmer and not indulge in the quagmire and sleaze world of spin-doctors. I do not want you tinkering with ideology that would infuse into you wrong philosophies about life and God."

## Dr. Alhasan Sisawo Ceesay, MD

My father came from a different generation with totally different perceptions about invaders ruling them. Let us for a moment step into their shoes to find out why the resistance for their progeny to attend school. In my father's days men believed in God, the sanctity of life and peaceful coexistence of the communities they lived.

About the invading longhaired men he calls devils, father said: "Son the way these men, meaning the colonialist, took over our countries can only be the work of the devil. They came from the blue sea and seized our land and minerals, and remaining on the best parts while leaving us the worst places to farm and for our animals to grace. To pour oil on fire they requested that we change our religions and ways to their dark and indiscipline life styles.

To top up, our people were forced to live under laws promulgated by the invaders on top of which we must pay to learn their languages while they make systemic concerted efforts to distorted and destroy everything that was dear to us.

They massacred, disgraced, and dethroned all our kings and chiefs. These shameful acts were reinforced with policies of divide and rule by pitting tribe against tribe and even bribing those bad elements willing to do their dirty work.

## After The Fall

Wages paid to workers were not worth the coin they were minted on. They made certain no organization, political or professional civil service existed in our countries". He said, "They filled the jails with those of us who refused to be indoctrinated or accept the supremacy of the foreign invaders.

So Son, because of kind heartedness and gentled nature of the African our ways are undermined and thrown out by invaders who replaced it with greed, unkindness, spin-doctoring, and lack of respect for man and nature. He concluded by saying, these are just a few reasons why I would not let my blood attend school".

The above is a pinhole view of father's radicalism and patriotic views. He did recap late later in his old age and finally gave full blessings to my efforts and future goals. He passed away peacefully to his maker in 1991 while I was a trainee doctor doing my clinical clerkship rotation at Colchester General Hospital in Colchester, Essex County, England.

Notices no matter how simple were just bundles of scribbles on worthless paper to the farmer. The illiterates who cannot decipher the prints are cheated of their rights and land.

Dr. Alhasan Sisawo Ceesay, MD

I was not going to be among those who cannot decipher the print and hence found my way to Kinte Kunda Primary School where I met with the head Master, Mr. Louis Albert Bouvier, who hailed from Banjul, our capital city.

This benevolent teacher was my first real contact with Western Education and we gelled instantly and became inseparable. He allowed me to stay at his home and treated me as his own son. He was kind and firm and wasted no time teaching me about life and on how to compete without strangulating the competitor.

Dr. Alhasan S. Ceesay holding Africa

## After The Fall

He told me repeatedly that competition was a healthy fund and stressed that one must be honest and have integrity and tolerance in life. He counselled hard work at everything one did. Above all, it was incumbent on me to have faith and to serve God daily, if not more but never less. Also he allowed me all the freedom a growing child needed without pampering me.

He did lay certain straightforward and simple rules for me. I was to study at a designated time, return home in time whenever I went into town, unless given an extension by him, and to be in bed by 10:00 pm, with lights off whether sleepy or not. He insisted that I perform my five daily prayers as expected of my religion even though he was devoured Catholic.

Mr. Bouvier would only help with my homework when he felt that I have done my best at it and that I was not trying to have him do the work. Otherwise, he would let me go and make a fool of myself before the class before I deserve his coveted help.

Hash you think but this strict beginning or treatment, as you would call it, made me do well at school and do things with confidence independently at very tender age.

## Dr. Alhasan Sisawo Ceesay, MD

I remain profoundly grateful to Mr. Louis Albert Bouvier for being educational springboard, for being a sincere and true friend and mentor. Something said by Francis Farmer summed up the relationship between L. A. Bouvier and me.

She said, "To have a good friend is the purest of all God' gifts, for it is a love that has no exchange of payments. It is not inherited, as with family. It is not compelling, as with a child. And it has no means of physical pleasures, as with a mate. It is, therefore, an indescribable bond that brings with it a far deeper devotion than others".

Mr. L. A Bouvier continued to help and mold my academic life until when I started Armitage School in 1957. Leaving a friend like Mr. Bouvier was difficult and emotional for both of us. We have become one and are now to say farewell and perhaps separate forever.

He prepared me well but like any parent or true friend he worried about the difficulties that lay ahead. I just wished they had transferred him with me to Armitage. On the day I boarded the land rover to Armitage tears rundown Mr. Bouvier's cheeks and mother turned her head away to hide her own.

## After The Fall

L. A. Bouvier was my best friend, after the loss of my twin brother, fate had it that I was now about to be far away from all I knew and loved. Mr. L. A. Bouvier kept cautioning me to, "keep your head up and do your school works. You have never been a failure, and even if such a sad experience occurs, keep trying over and over to overcome it.

We send you to Armitage with prayers, pride and above all with our deepest love. May God keep you in good health. Goodbye, Mr. Ceesay." It was very moving for this was the first time he addressed me as Mr. Ceesay.

We boarded the Land Rover and as it started to move Bouvier followed for some distance exhorting me not to fear to ask for help when need arose. He kept saying he would gladly help or would ask my parents to pitch in whenever possible.

Mr. L. A. Bouvier and I kept in touch despite the distance poor mail service of those days. The link continued while I was in the USA. I lost my friend in a motorcar accident, six year before returning from America in 1974.

His vehicle is said to have ran off the road went over a hill. Another part of me went with him. The evil that men do lives after them and the good is interred with their bodies.

Dr. Alhasan Sisawo Ceesay, MD

Well rest assured that L. A. Bouvier's good deeds did remain alive and intact on earth. At Armitage it was a newly qualified teaches from Kaur, Mr. Keko B. A. Manneh, who then doubled as our class' English and Mathematics teacher that filled in gap left by my leaving L. A. Bouvier at Kinte Kunda.

He was soft-spoken Chaucerian, a nickname we gave him because he crammed the entire work of Chaucer. He too loved me and was a good guide at Arbitrage. I am grateful for encouragement and help he gave and for really being there when I needed an honest person to open up to about difficulty or academic aspiration.

I left for New York on the 24 August 1967 and arrived at Alpena Michigan 1:30 Am on the 25 August 1967. Mr. Henry V. Valli, a counsellor and foreign student advisor at Alpena Community College, was at the bus station to pick me.

After the formality of welcoming to Alpena he drove me to 251 Washington Avenue the home of Mr. Howard Riggs where it had been agreed I stay until start of the semester in September before moving to Russell Wilson Hall at the Alpena Community College campus. Not surprising Mr. Valli and I became friends and remained so ever since.

## After The Fall

Mr. Howard Riggs and family welcomed me home as late as it was on that glorious day when I set foot in Michigan. They were all delighted to have me in their lovely home and they gave me princely meal to nourish my body and milk to quench my thirst.

Howard owned Ice-Cream Pallor down Town. He was very modest, delightful man and above all a very generous person. Soon Mr. and Mrs. Riggs became mom and dad throughout my American stay for their overwhelmingly kind people deserving such salutation from a poor villager.

Howard's warmth and generosity to other made his family unique company to foreign students coming to Alpena. The Riggs were the ideal Americans to me. They were average working family who readily shared the little bit God gave them with others less fortunate. I remained grateful to these kind-hearted friends.

Mr. Valli and Mr. Thomas Ritter, Director of Foreign students at Alpena Community College, and I met several time to discuss my financial nightmare. Mr. Ritter was too concerned that the college might face INS censor if he allowed my staying without a sponsor or means to pay fees and cater for myself.

Dr. Alhasan Sisawo Ceesay, MD

He was adamant and made it very clear to me that failure to get help for the first semester will leave him with no other option but to advise the immigration to consider deporting proceedings against me.

He gave a week ultimatum for me to sort things out before our next meeting 18 September 1967. Copies of letters from my future sponsor, Mr. Isdor Gold, never move or evoke sympathy from him as he epidermises a true inelastic bureaucrat.

Mr. Henry V. Valli convinced Mr. Thomas Ritter to hold on while get in touch with some residents about my case. He was on the telephone to different would be possible sympathizers to my cause.

Most of who agreed to contribute toward the cost of my first semester at Alpena Community College. Valli also spoke to the president of the college in my behalf to prevent Mr. Ritter from hastily and unilaterally contacting the INS for frivolous fears in his head.

My plight soon became a house whole affair and many residents pitched in to help resolve the case.

## After The Fall

The appeal by Mr. Henry Valli and Mrs. Viola Glennie snowballed letting me start my first semester at Alpena Community College, Alpena, Michigan. Fr. John miller at St. Bernard Rectory in Alpena not only lent me $250 but evangelized my state in every sermon for three weeks netting me much needed financial help.

God bless his heart. He left Alpena before my transfer to Olivet College in Olivet Michigan in 1979. Judge Philip Glennie was head of the 26$^{th}$ circuit Court of Michigan at the time. His wife, Mrs. Viola Gennie, was professor of foreign language at Alpena Community College.

Both not only contributed substantial amounts towards my tuition but also became my adopted parents in Alpena. They continued to link with me like wise support my goal until their return to heaven in the late nineties.

I remember these friends with joy mingled with sadness that they are not here to share reward they showed but also I remember them with intense gratitude for role and kindness shown me while a student at Alpena Community College, Alpena, Michigan, USA.

## Dr. Alhasan Sisawo Ceesay, MD

In another vein Alpena Community College gave me part time job at the Library and a summer job at the Salmon Experimental Fish hatchery. Thanks to grand efforts of Mr. Henry V. Valli and residents of Alpena I was able to overcome the financial crisis of my first semester at the college.

I met Mr. Cloyd Ramsey while seeking a summer job at the Medical Arts Clinic in Alpena. He was then manager of the unit at the time. Upon hearing my plight he promised to see what he could do even though the clinic itself had no jobs openings for that summer. I left him impressed and very moved by what he heard.

He too became an integral part of my time and sojourner in America than any through contributions and loans he took from the Alpena bank in my behalf to support my studies throughout my stay in the USA and short stay in Liberia, West Africa.

It was through kindness of Mr. Ramsey and his sponsorship that enabled Michigan Technological University at Houghton to accept me do a Masters program in Biological Sciences from 1971 to 1973.

After The Fall

L – R: Dr. Alhasan Ceesay, Prof. Sulayman Nyang, Mr. Cloyd Ramsey and Prof. Francis Conti

## Dr. Alhasan Sisawo Ceesay, MD

It was Mr. Cloyd Ramsey who came to my rescuer when things went very bad and unbearable and practically unsafe for me after the military coup d'etat against William Tolbert' administration of Liberia in 1981. He provided a round trip Air ticket to the USA and supporting it with invitation for me as their guest at Sandusky, Michigan December 1981.

The invitation secured me a B-2 Visa to Detroit, Michigan. I arrived in New York 1:15 pm 20 December 1981. I prayed on disembarking and I was grateful and thankful to God and Cloyd Ramsey having set foot once more on US soil. I thank Cloyd ceaselessly in my heart for having helped me escape to America despite the ignominy of being in exile and to seek asylum soon.

I caught my flight to Detroit, Michigan around 3:45 pm same day. The Ramseys were at the Detroit Metropolitan International arrivals terminal waiting to receive me. They must have noted the fatigue in my face, if not the sorrow of leaving my beloved Gambia and people behind for an indefinite time.

They welcomed me graciously and we headed for Sandusky, a small village in Michigan. I therein and then became part of the Ramsey family.

## After The Fall

Life has it that when some of us were created the mould broke. Most give their time and money to their own families or to work that brings them some happiness and some money. Cloyd Ramsey is among a few who give themselves wholly and unselfishly to others.

I can never be able to repay or tell how devoted Ramsey is in sharing life with the needy unless you meet him. In brief, Mr. Ramsey and wife Narrate fed and sheltered me when I needed food and place to stay until I get my feet back on earth.

He was my salvation voice in the wilderness of life's rugged road. I stayed as their guest in Sandusky until it was time to seek asylum at the Immigration and Nationality Service (INS) in Detroit. There was no other situation less tense and so empty of hope than this next phase in my life.

Life became an abyss of despair which only God and good friends, like the Ramseys, pulled me out from underneath. Shakespeare said, "Between the acting of a dreadful thing and the first motion; All the interim is like a phantasm, or a hideous dream. The genius and mortals instruments like to a little kingdom, suffers then the nature of an insurrection."

Dr. Alhasan Sisawo Ceesay, MD

Indeed an insurrection has been going on in my head during those horrible days of the coup d'etat of April 15$^{th}$ 1980 I became aware of the need to muster courage, strength and endurance to prepare myself for the coming exile days and form it may take.

Again, Mr. Ramsey contacted the Gambia several time to no avail to verify and correct a possible misunderstanding that may have occurred. Several friends and legislators Ramsey contacted advised that I seek asylum from the INS. Senator Carl Levin sent us a package of three copies of Form 1-589 for my use on 6$^{th}$ January 1982.

We took the bull by the horns, completed the forms and Ramsey and I proceeded to INS office at Mount Elliot Street, Detroit, Michigan on the 22$^{nd}$ February 1982, were I was subsequently interviewed separately and told action will be rendered in four months earliest.

If wishes were horses beggars would gallop to heaven for it took well more than eight months before any reply came and only after numerous INS court hearings did we get some semblance of partial positive direction. The final act was left with the State Department and vice president's office.

## After The Fall

Things were so delayed and difficult that I asked Ramsey to take me to the Catholic Mission for me to seek Sanctuary or more public help and support. We landed at St. Paul's' Cathedral, Diocese of Michigan, where Hugh Davis led me to the refugee office of the Diocese.

On hearing my story the refugee co-coordinator, Mrs. Patricia Koblinsky called rev. Hugh C. White, advisor to the reigning Bishop of the Diocese, Bishop Coleman Mcgehee Jr. The Diocese received and let me stay at 44 Ledyard Street in Detroit. In the mean time Ramsey sent the following appeal to the INS office at Mount Elliot in Detroit, Michigan:

TO WHOM IT MAY CONCERN

This letter is to acknowledge my association with Alhasan Ceesay, over a period of fifteen years. During that time I have found him to be a young man of very high ideals. His only interest in life has been to obtain an education and return to serve his home country and help his people.

I have personally invested thousands of dollars in Alhasan Ceesay because it seemed to me to be a very efficient way to help the impoverished people from his country that has had a great deal less than I have.

Dr. Alhasan Sisawo Ceesay, MD

If anyone were to follow the course of his life, he would see that his motives most certainly were not to simply escape the futility of his home country and live that, good life here. There is no doubt in my mind that the dangers that he describes do exist for him.

Even if these were less than perfect proof, would you like to take the chance of being wrong and find out that he had been imprison or worse killed for no reason at all? Please save this man. If you cannot do it for his sake, then consider the investment made by concerned individuals, other organizations and myself. Thank you for your serious considerations of this matter.

Signed: Cloyd Ramsey, Sandusky, Michigan, USA

My next Alpena Samaritan and brother in Chris as well as profession was Dr. Charles T. Egli, who I met almost about the same time I did with Ramsey. He was a Surgeon working for the Medical Arts Clinic at the time of our meeting. He came into the radar after a speech I gave to the Alpena Medical Association.

He too has contributed prominently and was instrumental in having the medical Association comes to my aid with a donation of $400 towards my second semester fees at Alpena Community College.

## After The Fall

By this miracle I was able to complete payment for the second semester at college. Charles, as he prefers being called, is a surgeon and devoted Christian who also became very close friend and had done a lot to encourage my efforts.

His rallying for assistance continued throughout his days at the Medical Arts Clinic. For you to note Dr. Egli's closeness here is a letter he sent in my behalf during my petitioning for asylum in the USA. It read:

Medical Arts Clinic

Alpena, Michigan

November 14, 1986

RE: Deportation Notice on Alhasan Ceesay

Dear Senator Levin,

Alhasan Ceeesay was a college student in Alpena many years ago when I first met him and was very much impressed by his sincerity and enthusiasm. He went onto graduate school at Michigan Technological University in Houghton, Michigan, in hopes of getting into medical school.

Dr. Alhasan Sisawo Ceesay, MD

He tried very hard to get into medical school in Africa. He was receiving no support from his own country because it considered him a political agitator and tribalist. Alhasan Ceesay on his own initiative was able to get into medical school in Monrovia Liberia and succeeded in taking two years medical education before he fled for safety to the USA.

He later sought political asylum in the USA for fear of persecution due to the aftermath of an attempted coup in July 181. It has always been his desire to complete his medical training and return to the Gambia when the climate warrants. For almost five years now, Alhasan has been trying to receive asylum, during which time his chances at medical school are affected. Most recently he received a letter from INS judge ordering his deportation. The deportation of Alhasan Ceesay back to the Gambia would result in his certain death or imprisonment and would constitute another tragedy in the way our government handles people like Alhasan. In a country where there are so many illegal aliens it seems that there must be some place for one more refugee. I beg you to personally consider Alhasan's case.

Sinerely

Dr. Charlse T. Egli, MD

## After The Fall

Mr. Homer Sheppard, resident of Flint Michigan, was also very kind to me while at Flint. He offered to lodge me during the summer of 1969 on securing a full time job at the St. Joseph Hospital on Flint, Michigan as nurse assistant.

Homer and wife offered to help defray rent expenses, which were taking a quarter of my earnings. With this help I was able to return to Alpena Community College at the end of the summer and pay my dorm and food bills and still had some pocket money to buy pens and other sundries during the semester.

God blesses his heart. We lost contact since my return to Africa. All letters to his address were redirected, as addressee no longer leaves here. Bishop Coleman Mcgehee had already blessed efforts of the hastily formed Ceesay Committee.

It became the Adhoc committee and my Pegasus wing. Like any normal human gatherings we had our different ideas as to how to approach the asylum problem but all of it steered towards or sought better ways to meet the challenges and enigma about to end all that I stood for and worked hard for in life.

Dr. Alhasan Sisawo Ceesay, MD

The brain storming sessions were very pragmatic if not practical and well-intended discussions. One of the exploratory searches for solutions led us to Mayor Harvey Sloan of Louisville, Kentucky.

I met Mayor Sloan in 1976 when I was trying to get into medical school at the University of Louisville. Also we used to write each other while I was in Monrovia, Liberia, West Africa. I was invited to his office early February 1983, and was given opportunity to talk with key aids at the Louisville City Hall while he attended other state affairs.

His executive aids, Sharon Wilbert and Mrs. Blanche reviewed my case along with information already in my file open in my name. They concluded that I did deserve help and I was asked to speak to Mrs. Joyce J. Rayzer, Director, and Health Affairs for the Mayor.

Joyce contacted the Dean of the Medical School and gave him an in-depth briefing of my background and precarious situation I was faced with. Two weeks later on February 28$^{th}$ 1983, I received the following letter from Joyce in behalf of Mayor Harvey Sloan. It read thus:

After The Fall

Office of the Director of Safety

City Hall

Louisville, Kentucky 40202

28 February 1983

Dear Mr. Ceesay,

It appears, as the old saying goes, that I have good news and bad news. I have been in contact with the University Of Louisville School Of Medicine with regards to your admission at the fall term. I have spoken to Dr. Donald Kemetz, Dean of the Medical School, and Mr. Harold Adams, Special Assistance to the president of the University of Louisville.

Both of these administrators upon reviewing the information you sent me feel that you are a very good candidate for the minority admission program. There is however, one issue, which must be resolved favourably before your admission to medical school, or the financing and packaging necessary to begging this endeavour can be given serious considerations.

The issue, which must be resolved, is the financial determination base on whether you would be granted asylum in the country.

Dr. Alhasan Sisawo Ceesay, MD

Without the asylum being granted and hence financial aid the university cannot proceed with your request for admission this fall because your legal status would be too tenuous for them to invest hard cash in your future medical development under such nebulous state.

It appears that you must begin medical school anew. The two years completed at Liberia, cannot be accepted for transfer. You will start as freshman upon being granted asylum in USA. Again, try and find resolution to granting you asylum.

I have been assured that everything that can be done for you will be done immediately upon a favourable notice of your asylum. Everybody in the Mayor's office says hello, and we are sending you our prayers.

Sincerely

Joyce J. Rayzer

Director, Health Affairs

This was the impact Mayor Harvey Sloan had. In addition Mayor Harvey Sloan sent the following directly from his desk to the INS pleasing for them to grant me asylum.

After the fall

City Hall

Office of the Mayor

Louisville, KY 40202

November 7, 1983

Alhasan S. Ceesay of the Gambia has contacted this office in an effort to gain political asylum in other to complete his medical education at the University of Louisville. I know that he is dedicated individual and is more desirous of providing needed medical aid to his fellow man.

Mr. Ceesay petitioned for political asylum in February 22, 1982 due to a purge, which followed a failed coup in the Gambia. The Medical school at the university of Louisville is currently processing his application for the 1984/85 academic years. It would be most helpful if you could assist him in expediting his papers.

He will not be admitted unless a written statement confirming his residency status is available. Since he has already lost two years awaiting residency confirmation, it would be deeply appreciated if you could assist this young man in any way possible. If my staff or I can be any further assistance in the matter, please do not hesitate to contact this office.

Dr. Alhasan Sisawo Ceesay, MD

Sincerely

Harvey L Sloan

Mayor Louisville

Let us for a moment revert to Bishop Coleman McGehee at the Episcopal Diocese of Michigan in Detroit Michigan. Below is letter sent to the INS director, Edwin Chauvin at Mount Elliot in Detroit, Michigan.

Office of the Bishop

4800 Woodward Avenue

Detroit, Michigan 48201

24 October 1983

Dear Mr. Chauvin,

As Bishop for the Episcopal diocese of Michigan, located in Detroit, Michigan, I write you this letter on behalf of Alhasan S. Ceesay, a petitioner for political asylum in the United States.

As you may note from the file Mr. Ceesay seeks political asylum base on his fear of political persecution and danger to his physical safety and well being by the government, were he to be returned by the INS to his country the Gambia.

## After The Fall

Mr. Ceesay's life will disclose to you, he was active opponent of the political regime in the Gambia. After protesting incarceration of his friends, Mr. Ceesay was placed on a list of individuals who were allegedly involved in criminal activity and who were involved with the Movement for Justice in Africa (MOJA) and were sought for interrogation by the Gambia government.

The Gambia government has singled our Mr. Ceesay because of his political opposition and has prevented him from continuing his medical education in Liberia by cutting off his financial assistance and by asking the Liberian government to return Mr. Ceesay to the Gambia. I am personally acquainted with Mr. Ceesay, and believe him to be an Individual who Is worthy of support of the Episcopal Dioceses of Michigan.

I feel that it took great courage for Mr. Ceesay to stand up for human rights and to publicly oppose the political regime in the Gambia. I am convinced that Mr. Ceesay is an altruistic individual who deserves to pursue his medical training to benefit, both in the United States and perhaps elsewhere, those individuals who might be helped by his medical ability.

Dr. Alhasan Sisawo Ceesay, MD

Mr. Ceesay has already establish his medical science aptitude in his studies at Medical School in Liberia, and he has applied to and been accepted by the School of Medicine at the University of Louisville, Kentucky, with tuition to be paid by that institution, upon his authorization to remain in the United States.

Mr. Ceesay has also sought authorization to engage in employment pending the outcome of his asylum request, he proposes to assist in medical research at the university should his employment authorization be granted by your office.

Therefore, on behalf of Mr. Ceesay as well as the members of my Diocese, I would urge you to give favorable consideration to Mr. Ceesay's petition and expedite his request for employment and his political asylum petition in every possible way so that his efforts to enter the University of Louisville School of Medicine may not be delayed any longer than may be necessary by legal and administrative procedures which you office follows.

Please feel free to contact me if I can be of any assistance in helping you to reach your determination on this matter.

After The Fall

I fervently believed that, upon your investigation of Mr. Ceesay's case, you would reach the conclusions that he would be an asset to the United States, and that his fears as to his persecution and personal safety should he return to the Gambia, have firm foundation in fact.

Very truly yours

(The Rt. Rev.) H. Coleman McGehee, Jr.

Bishop of Michigan

The Bishop of Michigan, H. Coleman McGehee followed the above with a letter to then vice president George Bush Sr. Who sent the following tars reply.

The Vice President

Washington, D. C

April 25, 1984

Dear Rev. McGehee,

Thank you for your recent letter concerning Alhasan S. Ceesay. It was thoughtful of you to write and I appreciate your having taken the time to bring Mr. Ceesay's case to my attention. I have asked the State Department to review all asylum cases and human rights violations, which are brought to my attention.

Dr. Alhasan Sisawo Ceesay, MD

I have, therefore shared your letter and the enclosures with officials at the Department of State and asked that they review Mr. Ceesay's request and write to you directly. I have also asked that a copy of their response be forwarded to my office. With best wishes

Sincerely

George Bush

Bishop McGehhee, Bishop Mason, Rev. Hugh C. white, Rev. David Brower, Rev. Bill Woods, Rev. Virgil Jones, and Rev. Mark D. Meyer all touched my heart in similar fashions Hence here is my collective feeling and experience in a nut shell about these devoted men of Christ.

All of the priests lived in Detroit, Michigan except Rev. Mark D. Meyer, who lived in Planes view, Texas, USA. I lived with Rev. Mark Meyer in 1989 after hurricane Hugo devastated our campus at Montserrat, West Indies. The rest of the above I met while trying to defray deportation notice from the INS. Those were challenging and nerving political moments for m family and I.

## After The fall

These men of God never docked when told about my nightmare. These true believers became unique brothers I would like to share few outstanding things they did in style engraved in simple devotion to Christ's dictum.

I write because these men impressed me in their interpretations and devotion to the Gospel of Christ. Hence forgive me if I became a bit sentimental in relaying help they gave to me at various challenging times of my life. They were personal pastors for me.

These were the beacon of hope and faith that stood by me when it was all doom and gloomy for me. They were simple people, humble ones at that, I can confide with, debate with, and had shoulders on which to cry my heart out without being embarrassed and above all expect a little prayer at the end of it.

Then guess what? We would be on tract trying to get hold of friends of theirs and people that might lighten my burden. Their devotion to justice and fairness was magnanimous and are my brothers in Christ. Rev. Mark Meyer, on being told the hardship I endured in Montserrat from hurricane Hugo gave me a room and gifts more than ten thousand us. dollars to help me complete my pre-clinics at the American University School of Medicine.

## Dr. Alhasan Sisawo Ceesay, MD

I learnt from these men of God that there is a special strength that can sustain us through almost any difficulty. That strength comes from God and from kind hearts like these Samaritans of good will. The strength comes from partly within but even more, it comes from faith and love of those close to us.

These men gave themselves wholly and as unselfishly to others in need when I met them at the Episcopalian diocese of Michigan. They devoted time to my cause and dropped selfish interests aside to help me fight my case against the INS while I was up to my neck in legal and political mud.

I found nothing in these men but admirable integrity, honesty and unswerving commitment to leading life devoted to God, the Bible and in helping the downtrodden.

I always feel elated whenever I get chance to speak to these kind hearts from afar. Meeting them makes me feel reunited with my best friends. I rather have a million more like then than multi millionaires that do not care about the plight of the common man. Again, I applaud contribution and friendship these men touched my heart and life with. God blesses them.

## After The Fall

My family, villagers and I are extremely indebted to them. These men translated their concerns, and love of humanity and continued to be my good Samaritans and a bridge over trouble waters. These believe in the worthiness and sanctity of life.

And above all they ascribe to the power of knowledge and justice over ignorance. We look forward to the day we can serenade them amongst us in the smiling coast of the Gambia. We pray they keep fit to be able to join us in the opening ceremony of the Manding Medical Centre at Njawara village, the Gambia, West Africa.

These men translated their deep faith, concerns, and love of humanity. I opted to do my clinical rotations in Colchester, Essex, UK in 1990 and chanced to meet the Robinson's. Keith Robinson vested my newly born baby girl, Famatanding Ceesay, at the Colchester County Hospital, which marked our first meeting.

This slightly shy bloke impressed me a lot. He was all smiles and fund. He titled the little ears of my daughter and told her not to be as bad as her daddy. We all laughed over it. We from that moment liked each other and he became one of my inseparable unique Brits.

## Dr. Alhasan Sisawo Ceesay, MD

Keith and wife would visit the Gambia and my girls loved them to bits. Not for the presents he takes to them each time but because of his amiable personality, altruistic, very caring human he is. He had spent boxes of monetary aid towards my NGO, Manding Medical Centre at Njawara village, and the Gambia.

On the forming of the Friends Manding Charitable Trust, he was unanimously voted chairman of the charity by the members. He had since inspiration of the Friends of Manding Charitable Trust worn the cap admirably and did a job well done for the charity.

Also he had been instrumental in the Gambibazaar held every fortnight in Colchester to help raise funds for Manding Medical Centre's goals back in the Gambia. He is committed to seeing the center come to fruition for the villagers of the Gambia and any that would need its service.

Personally, he and his wife had been my lifeline and support. They have always come to my aid the call of expectation and I remain profoundly grateful to him and his wife Lorna V. Robinson. Ten years ago I was on the verge of preparing becoming a consultant and return to serve the Gambia.

## After The Fall

Today an untold anguish my life went through in these years was dampened by kindness of Lorna and Keith Robinson and many other kind and generous Brits. They are my Colchester Samaritans and Njawara villager's angels with golden hearts.

We are working hard to seeing that Manding Medical center transcends the dream it was to reality for the Lower Badibou region. Its service is much needed by the villagers. God blesses their hearts. In Manchester many helped but few match Elhaj Asfaque Ahammed, Neville Brown, Kofi Awudo and Ahmed Nizami.

Ishfaque Ahammed is proprietor of Punjab Collection located at Wilmslow Road in Manchester. A lot has already been revealed about the kindness and generosity of this gentile heart and family in my first book, "The legend again all odds."

Ishfaque Ahammed has since my early days in Manchester to today been benevolent towards me. He gives me food and money any time he thinks or feels that I am on the brink of collapsing because of joblessness, hunger, and worries about the state of my equally beleaguered family back home. Only God can reward such humble good people.

## Dr. Alhasan Sisawo Ceesay, MD

I first met Neville in Montserrat, West Indies, while I was a medical student at the American University of the Caribbean. We have ever since been cordial and upon finding me out in Manchester he had steadfastly kept that friendship ablaze.

He in various ways would come to my aid with small but significant donations at the time. He even helped in securing a job at Belfry House Hotel at Hands Forth in 2006. He is kind hearted fellow and my Montserrat. Kofi Awudo is Toggles gentleman I also met through his link with Neville Brown. He turned to be very kind and generous to me. He bought me shoes and shirts to allow me start work at the above hotel.

Years later on my return from Glasgow, Scotland he was the one that lodged me free of charge for three winter months. He is of exceptional quality and humane person. I remain grateful both fellows. I met Mr. Ahamed Nizami in 2008, an angel in human flesh, at Waseem's work place in Manchester.

This lawyer turned Editor and I gelled from that hour to today. He is currently the Chief Editor of the Khalish Magazine, an Urdu language magazine in UK and worldwide. He also doubles as one of the Pakistani group leader in Manchester. On knowing my predicaments his benevolence surfaced.

## After The Fall

There nod then he promised to help me with some the problems pulling me down and also indicated interest in helping my NGO Manding Medical Centre get financial aid to get a head start on the provision of its goals for the villagers.

In addition he proposed a fun raising idea using his medium and other avenues that may come to light. We tentatively initiated, depending on approval and provisos set by Keith Robinson, Chairman of Friends of Manding Charitable Trust in Colchester been met, formation of the Manchester manding Medical Center Annex to be office at 9 knowley Street in Manchester.

To further demonstrate his kindness and interest in my goal Ahmed Nizami donated fees for all three PLAB exams I took in 2009. Gentle hearts like Ganem Hadied and others felt sorry that my life became an unkind and rough ride for me. He said, "Ceesay, I wish I can help more to get you out of the limbo you found yourself. Just believe in God and this pain will one day pass like history."

Mahmud Adam also marched Ganem's effort by collecting money from the Liverpool mosque. Both monies were used for my exam fees and for which kindness I remain eternally grateful to all donors.

Dr. Alhasan Sisawo Ceesay, MD

Mohamed Salam of Greenhey business in Manchester was another Good Samaritan that came to my aid when I was left to sleep in cold weather at Alexandra Park. Upon contacting him he kindly offered me room in one of his flats in Manchester.

He was very kind and generous towards me. We have many times prayed together for my eventual breaking out of nightmarish bad luck life had been to me in recent times.

Last but not the least is Sami Bati from Algeria who I stayed with at 245 Great Western Street and who relentlessly called and ask people and friends to come to aid. He raised a bundle to help me pay school fees for my daughters in the Gambia and feed my bones.

My brother Abdullah Hashim and wife Asiya Qadri were very kind Bangladesh cum Pakistani couple I met during the most challenging times of my life. Their kindness is yet to be matched by their peers. I met the couple while sleeping rough in the street of Manchester as Mohamed Salam' offer of a place came to an abrupt end.

## After The Fall

The place was rented to a family leaving me homeless with no place to go except spend the nights at cold and treacherous Alexandra Park. It was very risky but being jobless it was the only option left to me. Hence, it was a miracle when this God fearing Good Samaritan couple came to my rescue.

They not only lodged me temporally at their other flat at 2 Sway field in Manchester but also continued to shower me with gifts and food. I certainly look forward to hosting and having my villagers and family serenade this unusually kind and generous couple from Bangladesh.

Yankuba Samateh and dear friend Abdinsir Hassan deserve a mention with gratitude and thanks for kindness and generosity they showered me with during these dark days and for constantly reminding me that I am more than capable of bringing my dream to fruition for the villagers.

Mrs. Yata Corr-Sey, a cousin, remained the most supportive and one that kept encouraging me more than any family member had done during this sojourn of mine. God blesses her and her family.

I look forward to being able to thank her in person for insisting that blood is thicker than water and for being with me in thick and thin of this murderous trail.

## Dr. Alhasan Sisawo Ceesay, MD

I just have to have continued faith; confidence to do it and the universe will cooperate to justify these days difficulty. My life being as mythical as Pelebstine fever, it was full of ups and downs and again it was Ahamed Nizami who offered to lodge me when I was asked to leave my previous address where I was renting. His kindness is phenomenal and transience's mortals.

I look forward to him being my guest in the Gambia. Worth mentioning is Abdullah Shahim, a young Bangladeshi fellow who practiced his believe that we are all God's children and do need to help the "miskin" whenever we can.

He has graced my life with kindness and brotherhood that any human being yearns to get. He and his wife Asiya Padri have been one of the bright experiences of my UK sojourn. God bless their hearts. Asiya is a shining beauty and sunshine of Abdullah Shahim.

Each day became a specific thrill that lead to that exhilarating moment of victory for mankind. It was a hard challenge and a march placed before me. It is a march I will pursue towards the day I would once again be able to serve the Gambia as a physician.

## After The Fall

Friends such as Lorna Robinson, Eliza Jones, Mahmud Adam, Ganem Hadied, Abdinnisir, Faisal, Yusuf Ali, Ishfaque Ahmed, Ahmed Nizami, Abdullah Shahim, and countless angels all suffered my pain and felt way into my heart through compassion as I plied through financial inadequacies.

Angels like Faisal, Abdul Rhaseed, Abdinnisir, Yusuf Ali, and Mahmud Adam deserved to be classed as paragons of kindness. These Somalis are among many who refused to let me bit the dust because of foot dragging visa problem. They encouraged by sharing food and they had with me and made certain that I persevere for a bright day for family and country. These are people who help lift my feet when my wings could not remember how to fly away from hardship.

Faisal would on weekends prepare hot and well spiced Spaghetti and meat, or buy food for me from the next door restraint. Abdinnisir Hassan in almost tearful manner would push me into going to get food.

On top of this generosity these folks let me stay in their flat at 284 Great Western Street, Manchester while my lawyer fight not only to untangle but to get the Home office act on change of status request I made to that office back in 2004.

Dr. Alhasan Sisawo Ceesay, MD

I feel favoured, if not blessed having to face these inhuman challenges without losing my sanity. Being in the belly of a ferocious beast is more comfortable than life I am currently saddled.

I feel like being at the interface between Purgatory and hell on earth. Simply put, my experience was no domain for the weak. The dilemma in this life remains ceaselessly changing. These few, this band of altruistic brothers kept me going through many a dark hour of my life in America and Great Britain.

They stood tall for me among many in caring for the plight of those who they never met in poverty stricken parts of the world. Friends like these are angels who lift us to our feet when our wings have trouble remembering how to fly.

In this almost inhospitable life friends like these are a great gift indeed. Tinged with trepidations for what the future can sing I picked up courage and inspiration knowing that good comes out of fighting for what one believes in.

Life has taught me how to look after myself and that things do not just happen, people make it happen. And so the villagers and I appeal for your help and participation with Manding Medical Centre.

## After The fall

Together we can walk on water and make this dream of providing medical aid to villages become worthy cause for generations. I have learnt not to rest on my oars else I fall into a deep and turbulent sea of troubles.

I have to keep running in order to be with the best or where I am. I will continue to not only learn to improve my performance but to work hard to see that this dream of providing a much needed medical aid to villagers is brought to fruition.

Dalliance said, "Say of me what you will and the morrow will judge you, and your words shall be a witness before its judgment and a testimony before its justice. I came to say a word and I shall utter it. Should death take me ere I give voice the morrow shall utter it. That which alone I do today shall be proclaimed before the people in the days to come."

Brother Dudou Ceesay, in green, with family

Dr. Alhasan Sisawo Ceesay, MD

Chapter 24

I REST MY CASE

Paul in a letter to Timothy 2 said, "I have fought a good fight, I have finished my course, and I have kept the faith." I hand this work for publication for you to be judge of the ravages of the years and how my life was that of extreme ups and downs.

In reality, I am very grateful to God even though my life met with various misfortunes, the most unbearable being the delay in my becoming a physician.

My life as witnessed in these pages was an assembly of trials and tribulation emanating from roadblocks placed on my path by inhuman laws and unfortunate dark circumstances.

Life has taught me to submit to divine decrees, whatever they may be from God. I feel on the whole overly rewarded and delivered even though I had no family here in England nor was I as lucky as others who can feel and experience the warmth of their wives and children on daily basis.

I succumbed to it as the way things were going to be for me and lived with this state of affairs while in Manchester, England. I experienced various turns of fate, enough for ten elephant loads, while on the little moat of the silver sea called England.

## After The Fall

With my travels I was able to see Europe, the Americas and have learnt a great deal from it as well as experienced numerous unforeseen adventures thrown on my path. My life in England was pain; fear of deportation, hunger, extreme poverty due to joblessness, solitude and missing my wife and children I loved dearly.

I had a huge sense of duty in relation to the villagers and was not ready to fail them because of personal comfort or pleasures. Consequently Manding Medical Centre and benefits to be accrued from it became my most if not the only occupation and direction in life.

Here is Manding Medical Centre if managed well it will do justice to rural health service for the next generation of Gambians to build upon. The medical centre is now a recognized charity in both the United Kingdom and America. I am committed to serve the villagers so that life of the children and young people would be better than mine when I was young.

I hope Manding Medical Centre becomes a model testimony of the boy from Njawara village who doggedly struggled to become a doctor and despite various twists of life is able to provide medical aid and service to villagers in rural Gambia.

May be this will strengthen some other fellow to strive to do better than I did to bring health and happiness to the region. I hope my adventure persuades youngsters that man is capable of a lot more than he thinks he is capable of.

## Dr. Alhasan Sisawo Ceesay, MD

Our footprints must be inspirational to give heart to new coming Gambian generations. Twenty years ago none would dream of thinking me becoming an author or to challenge powers as I did in this little frame and life of mine. I met a beautiful Maraka girl while I was in Monrovia, Liberia, West Africa. Fatou Koma is daughter of Elhaj Ansuman Koma and Jalian Ture of Kindia from Guinea Conakry.

Her positive attitudes towards me lead our meeting on weekends at Cousin Sainabou Jobe's home. We started going out together and very soon I had the courage to ask her hand in marriage. There was no bone of contention with regards for my love for her. She was the darling of my heart at first sight and I was not going to let a fly land on her from that day onwards.

We had a simple wedding because her father did not quite approve of me because of fear for his uneducated but very pretty daughter being dump at one stage of the marriage for another educated city girl.

I, in the long run, allied his fears and he ended up being one of my best friends and confidants I had up to the day he went to his maker.

Fatou Koma-Ceesay and I are blessed with three beautiful daughters namely, Princesses Famatanding Ceesay, Binta Ceesay, and Roheyata Ceesay. All of who, unlike me, had their schooling start at the age of five. The elder girl is aspiring to become a doctor and had been admitted to start her premed courses at Alpena Community College in Alpena, Michigan, USA.

## After The Fall

Together Fatou Koma-Ceesay, the children and I went through all the tragedy of hunger, poverty and other sad experiences my sojourn in the quest of the Golden flees for the villager brought to us. Fatou Koma-Ceesay initially hated Manding Medical Centre for she felt it consumed me and took me away from her and the children. The call got me entangled in a web of unfortunate circumstances and laws. The marriage had at one point almost spiraled to its end as wife' move became questionable.
Nonetheless she remained a good mother and wife who took care of the girls in my absence. My mother in-law was battered by confusion and as to why Fatou stuck it out with me under such immense hardship. Love is stronger glue! We loved each other and so we were able to stand by the other in good or bad times and my trip to England was the worst ever in our connubial life.
It caused great turbulences in the marriage but I stuck with it for love's shake and the children who I love dearly. Today, we are back together as family under the same roof while planning and supporting future of our darling girls. God bless Fatou Koma-Ceesay's heart and be reassured of endless love I have for her.
For now Dalliance said it best for me when he said, "Say of me what you will and the morrow will judge you, and your words shall be a witness before its judgment and a testimony before it justice.

## Dr. Alhasan Sisawo Ceesay, MD

I came to say a word and I shall utter it. Should death take me ere I give voice; the morrow shall utter it. That which alone I do today shall be proclaimed before the people in days to come." I wrote with the hope the life enshrined herein will serve not only as an inspiration to the despondent but a lesson never to allow this sort of experience it passed through this planet.

I wrote in the hope that life enshrined in my books will serve not only as an inspiration to the despondent and downtrodden but a lesson never to allow this sort of experience it passed through this planet. I wrote because I felt that my life has something worth revealing to the world to engender tolerance and understanding between people and their governments.

I risked revealing today for all of us to learn from it and move to a better and rewarding future. Among the forces of life is one that stands a certain lofty peak a few is endowed with or able to explore its heights. Ambition urges us to leave the lower surface of earth where the ordinary people live and ascend to heights that pierce the heavens.

This mission has led to numerous Erie paths but for me this Pell-mell towards a better medical service for the neglected villager was a worthwhile adventure. I am profoundly grateful and indebted to my wife Fatou Koma-Ceesay and our daughters, princesses Famatanding Ceesay, Binta Ceesay and Roheyata Ceesay for enduring all the pains that we went through in thick and thin times during my sojourn to America and England.

After The Fall

Also my deepest gratitude goes to Cousin Yata Sey-Corr for helping keep my family hopeful. God bless her heart eternally. I forgive my own brothers and sisters who refused to cater for my family in my absence. Hello, hats off to Sey kunda!

Dr. Alhasan Ceesay, holding Africa

# Dr. Alhasan Sisawo Ceesay, MD
## Chapter 25

### MY ENDEARING LIFE & FATE

For a while in my native innocence all I had was erudition and wit, which always misfired. Everything I touched came to nothing but failure, whatever I tried to achieve came crashing down on my head. At any given moment some mishap befalls me and nothing surprised me any more.

I took my current plight with stride and smiled as fate taunts me. I remain poor but my in extinguishable strong will enabled me face life squarely and took me through these dark days. The twist of fate abated but my age had advanced beyond retrieval. The above apocalyptic life is indeed trying moments for my family and me. The only passion I have is providing medical service to villagers through Manding Medical Centre.

My dream spawns better future health service for future generations. I never set to write a bestseller but to inform and share ideas. Also I enjoy reading it as it's not found in any bookstore. It is hoped that in writing another will be spared of experienced I endured before being able to provide medical service/aid to Gambian villagers. Browse: http://friendsofmandinggambimed.btck.co.uk or contact alhasanceesay@hotmail.com To view/purchase books: Google search Dr. Alhasan Ceesay/ books.

# After The Fall

Dr. Alhasan S. Ceesay, MD

Dr. Alhasan Sisawo Ceesay, MD

Chapter 26

THE WAY OF A DREAMER

Back in the Gambia a friend decried my efforts as nothing but a dream that I persistently chased. I let such observers know that it only takes time before my dream become fruitful. Here are a few examples: I left the Gambia in 1967 as a nurse and returned; after insurmountable roadblocks as a medical doctor.

While practicing in the Gambia I further created two worthy entities, namely (1) The Gambia Health Credit Union, which today provides needed financial assistance to all health workers i.e. Nurses and Health Inspectors country wide. (2) In addition I created NGO Manding Medical Centre at Njawara village, Lower Badibou to help provide a much needed medical aid and service free of charge to villagers who could not afford to pay private clinics. With the help of visiting doctors the centre has treated more than 9000 villagers free of charge since its inception in 1993.

On returning to the UK, I again with help of resident nurses and doctors in Colchester Essex setup the Friends of Manding Charitable trust in Colchester UK. This was recognized and registered as a charity in England and Wales by the UK- charity Commission in 2002.

## After The Fall

In the midst of which I published my first book 'The Legend Against all Odds' and now has published more than thirty eight novels. To further cement my goal for the villager I was able to convince the Alpena City Council to form a sister city link with Njawara and Kinte Kunda villages in the Lower Badibous of the Gambia in 2005. This was made easier after my being awarded on May 5th, 2005 'Distinguished Graduate Award' by Alpena Community College. My web site: friends of Manding gambimed continues to lure people to Njawara to see what help they could give the villager.

Today, I am not only an author of several books; Google search: Dr. Alhasan Ceesay/books to view of purchase as contribution to rural healthcare; portions or sales from these books go to support goals of Manding medical Centre at Njawara. I am indeed a dreamer and will continue to dream fir my people.

If the above is dream then here is another step to help see through me. I am humble to let you know I am now a Publisher and my company in the UK is 'PUBLISH KUNSA LTD' and one can have their work published by logging on to our web site: www.publishkunsa.com. Again two pounds sterling from any book published by my company goes towards scholarships and rural healthcare as stipulated in terms of contract we would work on manuscripts. Dreams must be activated and not wasted.

## Dr. Alhasan Sisawo Ceesay, MD

I cannot fly without wing but can make artificial wings to let reach higher hits that loafers never can dream of. Allow the dream to force you into action. Yes, I too have a dream, which is simply that every hamlet in the Gambia be bequeathed good healthcare, safe drinking water, enough food and chance to a solid education for every child.

Yes. Education is power and a mover. I sacrificed my life to endure depravity, humiliation and solitude in other to bring medical aid to villagers. With all these I am busy trying to get more medical skills and experience before heading to Gambia, home , sweet home.

With this tit-bit I can freely and willingly encourage you to dream but not to let it remain at that. A life with trials or challenge is like an orchestra without conductor and it very defeating if not boring indeed. One must act for the good of self and any community we find ourselves.

An old village sage once advice that 'A good person and at best a leader never yield to failure but only learns from it to move forward. Grand Pa Bajoja Ceesay told me that; "One willing to do good should not expect people to remove obstacles or stones from their path; but such leaders must accept it calmly in the event these place more boulders on our way."

## After The Fall

This is what a dream turns out. At first it becomes a lonely avenue full of heartaches, which eases gradually as the good things unfold from one's relentless efforts to make the dream becomes fruitful and rewarding.. Simple its life 99.9% very hard work full of stumbling.

Do not we all dream of going to heaven? Well the path to such respites need challenging theological and spiritual discipline. Hence we earthly dreamers dabble with ideas of landing on Mars and eventually colonizing it. So allow me ask, what is your dream for mankind, especially Africa?

Can Africa ever be free of ignorance, self subtenant, corruption and misuse of the tribe? These just few multipronged toxic dragon heads African must dream to remove from our midst. With better education and discipline Africa can overcome and progress. Dreamers are doing utmost to slay the pestilent dragon hindering life in the villages of rural Africa.

We must remove the monster of retro ration for the shake of the future generation. Again grandpa Bajoja Ceesay advices that we stay the good cause and never be taken by detractions. I am no millionaire but have a million dreams worthy of pursuing for my people. Would you dream along with me? Glad to let you know hard work yields rewarding fruits.

## Dr. Alhasan Sisawo Ceesay, MD

Dream and be in control of not only your own life but be a source of hope and inspiration while contributing positively to your community. Do not be carried along by current get rich quick and live selfishly. Life is to be shared even with dreamers. Time is not mine and life will continue for the villager. Success comes slowly and brings with it contagious hope that serves as blue print for other.

The fate of mankind is up to each of us. Do not succumb to idleness. Use youthful opportunity to develop out of ignorance, and corruption by having courage to bring change to the people. Be the change you want in others. Expect resistance on your path to bring change. A useful proxy in fulfilling a dream is not letting it wane away. Always think it possible and work hard at its realization.

Be warned to think what could be done and not that which cannot be archived. Matrix of success lies in hard work with guided ski full knowledge. I will work on my dream and morrow will be my judge along with benefits accrued from it. I hope my last footprints of my journey on earth will inspire people towards doing well and sharing their worth with others. From one villager to another may this wish be true for rural Gambia.

After The Fall

Chapter 27

ABOUT THE AUTHOR

I was born at Njawara Village, Lower Badibou District in the North Bank of the Gambia. I am a scion of a Mandinka and Fulani tribe and am one of five siblings. I had my education at Kinte Kunda, then Armitage High School, ending up as a registered nurse at the Royal Victoria Hospital, Banjul, before embarking to the USA on my medical degree quest.

I graduated from the American University School of Medicine in Montserrat, West Indies, in 1992 and returned to the Gambia to start setting up a self-help village health NGO Manding Medical Centre. The Gambia Government and the Badibou local authority register NGO Manding Medical Centre.

The centre has treated more than 9000 patients free. I am married to Fatou Koma-Ceesay and we are blessed with three beautiful girls, Famatanding Ceesay, Binta Ceesay and Roheyata Ceesay. Unlike me, all of them started school early without the roadblocks I had to cross in my early years.

I am currently a medical officer at the Royal at the Royal Victoria Hospital on study leave.

Dr. Alhasan Sisawo Ceesay, MD

It is my hope that this work will inspire others and bring much needy help to providing medical service to rural Gambia. You are urged to log onto:

www.friendsofmandinggambimed.btck.co.uk ; or www.publishkunsa.com to learn more about my work with villagers. Dear reader I hope you enjoyed navigating through the piece of work I am contribute for all of us makes case for change in attitudes of government and the governed.

For now, Dalliance said it best for me when he said, "Say of me what you will and the morrow will judge you, and your words shall be a witness before its judgment and a testimony before its justice.

I came to say a word and I shall utter it. Should death take me ere I give voice, the morrow shall utter it. That which alone I do today shall be proclaimed before the people in days to come."

I wrote with the hope the life and position enshrined herein will serve as not only an inspiration to farmers, the despondent but also a lesson never to allow these shameful international jigsaw games continue as experience to pass through this planet.

After the fall

I felt that it is worth writing about the above because it is something worth revealing to honourable men and women to engender change, tolerance and understanding between people and governments. I risked speaking out for all of us to learn from it and move forward to a better and rewarding future.

Dr. Ceesay & Wife Fatou Koma-Ceesay
Colhchester, Essex, 2000

Dr. Alhasan Sisawo Ceesay, MD

Have your manuscript become a book by submitting it for possible publication to acquisitions@publish Kunsa. Com

PLease contact us to expose your work globally.

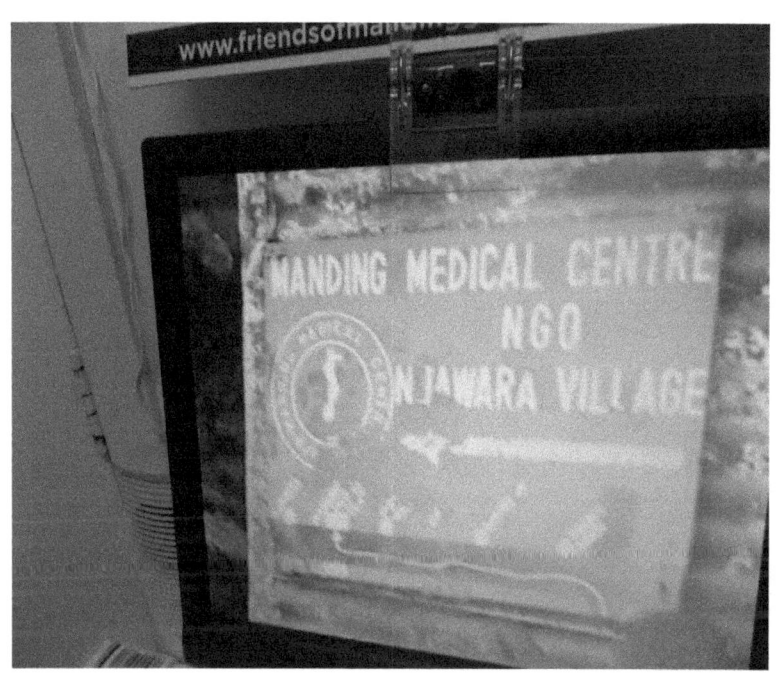

www.ingramcontent.com/pod-product-compliance
Lightning Source LLC
Chambersburg PA
CBHW071145160426
43196CB00011B/2016